First printing: November, 2023

Printed in the United States of America

For information regarding publicity for author interviews, contact Thomas R. McDonald, Sr., at boomac222@aol.com

BOOMER REFLECTIONS

I REMEMBER A BETTER AMERICA

By

Thomas R. McDonald, Sr.

CONTENTS

INTRODUCTION

Turning 65 in modern America tends to create a spirit of reflection. After all, this is the age when Americans could register with the federal government's Medicare healthcare system, the traditional age of work retirement, and the official age of becoming a "mature senior citizen." My first thought when becoming this age was "I can't believe I'm this old!" My second thought was "Thank God, I AM this old!"

I was blessed to be born to wonderful Christian parents in the spring of 1957, during the peak of the historical "baby boom" generation, in Memphis, Tennessee. These wonderful parents (Tom & June) were right out of a "greatest generation" novel. They both survived the hardships of the Great Depression during their childhoods, the sacrifices of World War II and the Korean War during their youths, and both managed to have decent white-collar middle-class careers with no higher education. It was not easy to raise three very "active" boys all about the same age on a limited income during the crazy 1960s and 1970s, but they both believed in the American dream, and they certainly believed in a higher power.

I have also been blessed to have two wonderful brothers (one older, one younger) who were clearly my best friends over the years, and the good fortune to live and work in my beloved central Arkansas most of my life. After my younger brother died suddenly in September, 2007, I have learned that we must never, ever, take a day of living for granted. My many business, political and social friends have also taught me a lot of important life lessons over the years, and many of these unique words of wisdom and   true stories will be discussed in this book.

Even though I have had the privilege to receive about eight years of college education that have provided a solid foundation for learning, I now consider the best lessons of life to be learned from other people who have been engaged in my life…family, friends, work peers, teachers, and clients. And, of course, we all learn a lot from our careers and jobs, regardless of the specific fields.

My long and varied work journey started as a pizza cook and backroom prep man at a popular pizza parlor at the tender age of

14. I remember how excited I was to receive my very first "real paycheck" that summer. The federal minimum wage was a whopping $1.60 per hour. My older brother, who helped me get the job, laughed out loud when I popped this brilliant question: "Who is this FICA guy? He just stole money out of my first paycheck!" In later years I have worn many job hats… grocery clerk, sales rep, supervisor, public relations manager, compliance investigator, city councilman, teacher, businessman, landlord. Each of these job roles taught me unique and valuable life lessons, including how to be a good American.

I dedicate this book to all the smart and kind people that have tolerated my professional and personal journey over these many years and have helped me along the way to become a proud and happy American. A special thanks, also, to my best friend in life, my sweet wife Becky.

CHAPTER 1

The Early Years – Spring 1957

PEAK OF "BABY BOOM" POPULATION EXPLOSION

I have often heard over my lifetime that "there is no such thing as luck." I respectfully disagree. In May, 1957, I was extremely lucky to be born in the United States of America. As an added lucky bonus, I was born into a wonderful Christian home headed by Tom and June McDonald in Memphis, Tennessee, during the peak of the American "baby boom" population explosion. Those were the famous "happy days" during the second term of the Eisenhower/Nixon administration, as portrayed by popular TV shows and movies that highlighted the beginning of care-free youthful rock-n-roll, hot rods, drive-in diners and movies, and included legendary TV shows such as "American Bandstand," "Leave it to Beaver," and "Father Knows Best." Even though I could not remember those early years, of course, my sweet parents often reminded me and my two brothers that although those "happy days" were indeed fun in many ways, there were also many other very serious events happening around the country and the world.

Early in 1957, President Eisenhower announced the famous "Eisenhower Doctrine" that pledged defense of eastern nations against the spread of communism. The United States conducted the first underground nuclear test later that summer, and in September of that year the president ordered federal troops to enforce racial integration of public schools at Central High School in Little Rock, Arkansas. I could never have imagined that I would have the opportunity of meeting the very first African American graduate of Central High, Mr. Ernest Green, in person in the fall of 2012 while working as a school administrator there. In October, 1957, international events became really serious for our country. The Soviet Union launched the world's first artificial satellite named "Sputnik" that started the international "Space Race." This was a real game changer for America, both good and bad. The race for space created a new sense of national urgency and patriotism, in conjunction with many positive technology-related economic developments. However, this major global event also intensified the Cold War-related arms race with the Soviets and their military allies that became very dangerous, complex, and extremely expensive for the taxpayers. President Eisenhower publicly warned our citizens often about the long-term negative effects of the "military industrial complex."

When the rocket technology of the 1950s combined with the atomic/nuclear bomb technology of   the 1940s, it created a new serious problem for mankind: ICBM's (Intercontinental Ballistic Missiles.) The whole world had already witnessed the devastation of the American atomic bombing delivered by airplanes upon Japan on August 6th and 9th, 1945, which ended World War II. With ICBM's, people across the globe could reasonably envision the horrors of nuclear weapons being delivered by high-speed missiles flying across oceans – and with very little notice. Since both world's "superpowers" (USA & Soviet Union) had developed these massive operational weapons, both sides decided that they had to keep their ICBM production at least equal to the others for their own safety and national defense. These mutual national defense strategies created the worst and most expensive arms race in world history, and it also tied directly into the new global space race. Most baby boomers can remember the "drop-and-duck" drills they regularly practiced at their public schools during   the Cold War era. In conjunction with fire and storm drills, school kids across America would practice what they should do in the event of a nuclear bomb attack. During a typical school day, students would pretend to hear a public alarm/siren. They were told to hide under their desks and cover their heads with their hands….as if those flimsy small desks would save them when a massive powerful Soviet ICBM zoomed into central Arkansas. A nuclear bomb attack was a real fear when I was a young grade school kid. Arkansas at the time had several of the first generation "Minute Man" missile silos installed in the central and northern parts of the state and we learned that those missile silos would probably be toward the top of the Soviet target list! In later years, the federal government began updating those missile locations with the next-generation "Titan" missiles that even prolonged our fear of being at the top of the attack target list. But, life went on, especially for us kids.

At the same time that these very serious international political events were transpiring, the American "happy days" social culture kept rolling along. Elvis Presley became the "king of rock-n- roll" and bought the now-famous Graceland estate in Memphis. My Dad always had a sentimental feeling for Elvis because he graduated from the same Humes High school in Memphis back in the mid- 1940s. Even though he preferred classic singers like Frank Sinatra, Perry Como, and Tony Bennett, he appreciated Elvis's amazing voice and humble beginnings. Classic '50s rock tunes such as "Jailhouse Rock," "Wake Up, Little Susie," and "That'll Be the Day" were at the top of the music charts. The amazing classic plays of "West Side Story" and "The Music Man" were big Broadway hits in New York.

The Brooklyn Dodgers moved to Los Angeles, and the New York Giants moved to San Francisco, changing the landscape of "America's pastime" (major league baseball.) The now-famous "frisbees" were first introduced to provide simple and inexpensive fun for kids during outdoor events. In other words, even though the world was quickly becoming very dangerous and complex during the late 1950s, and the Cold War was becoming warmer every day, the American spirit remained strong and vibrant. Most folks in those days were very proud to be Americans, land of the free and home of the brave. But, of course, everything was far from perfect. The United States Congress approved the first significant civil rights legislation since the Civil War, and clearly not all Americans had the same opportunities. But, the basic family structure and work ethic for most Americans were without a doubt stronger before the advent of the tragic "welfare culture" of the 1960s.

In the meantime, my young parents had their hands full during these historic times. My younger brother (their third son) was born in May, 1958, which again landed near Mother's Day, shortly after Dad accepted a job transfer with a major railroad company, moving us from Memphis to Little Rock. Mom often told us this story about how my brother and I were both born near back-to-back Mother's Days. The nurses at the Little Rock hospital asked Mom: "Hey, Mrs. Mac, how in the heck did you manage to give birth to two bouncing baby boys near back-to-back Mother's Days?" Mom's response: "Well, I guess I am just a very good scheduler."

I remember asking both my sweet parents, when I was learning American history in school, about this unique time. The more I learned about the seriousness of the Cold War, I wondered how they managed the daily fear factor - what did they do to protect themselves? Were they involved in the public debate? Did they listen to all the cool '50s Elvis and other rock-n-roll tunes? My dad always listened to us and always respected our opinions, even as somewhat naïve kids at the time. He was a veteran of both the US Coast Guard at the end of World War II, and the US Army during the Korean War era, even though he never experienced actual combat. He was the classic "compassionate conservative" and a devout "tolerant Methodist," soft-spoken and an avid reader of history. His basic and respectful response to me, when I asked, was memorable when I was a teenager: "Well, son, that's a very good question. That was a scary time in history, especially in October, 1962, during the Cuban Missile Crisis. We did not have much spare time on our hands in those days to be afraid or to get involved in public discussion. We really had to focus on just making a living, getting the bills paid, and keeping you boys fed – which, as you know, was a significant challenge."

It was not the "profound" parental answer I was hoping for, but then a light came on in my head. My dad's answer to this question was probably similar to most young parents of the baby boom generation. Most honest and hard-working Americans have never had time to sit around and dwell on their fears and problems – they lower their heads and work through their problems with courage and dedication – they do what it takes to get the job done. America was founded on "rugged individualism" and a never-ending thirst for FREEDOM! Most of us do not desire a government handout. We want the liberties and opportunities to pursue "happiness" that our brilliant American founding fathers envisioned many years ago.

I cannot ever remember a PERFECT America,

but I do remember a BETTER America!

CHAPTER 2

The Crazy 1960s

Much has been written, discussed, and broadcasted about the very unique historical, political, and social events of the 1960s in America. Historians have described this decade as "turbulent," "radical," "bizarre," "tragic," "wild," and even "inspirational." I believe that just "crazy" would suffice. From my baby boomer viewpoint, this decade basically represents my young childhood innocence and disillusionment from my earliest memories of these major events, from kindergarten through grade school.

The 1960 presidential election between Republican Vice President Richard M. Nixon and Democrat US Senator John F. Kennedy was intriguing. Nixon was still generally popular with many Americans as he rode the political coattails of President

Eisenhower, but Senator Kennedy was younger and more energetic with a "million-dollar" smile, and he demonstrated exceptional speaking skills during the now-famous national TV debates that propelled him to a razor-thin victory. I was still too young to actually remember this historic election that ended in controversy in Cook County, Chicago, Illinois, but I do remember, when I was in kindergarten, my middle-of-the-road conservative parents discussing their disappointment. As a service veteran, my dad really "liked Ike" (mirroring the well-known campaign slogan.) He admired Eisenhower's strong military leadership during World War II and his calm demeanor of peace and prosperity throughout those 1950s "happy days." He viewed VP Nixon through similar lenses, and was frustrated that Americans voted for   style over substance.

An event I also remember as a young child was my parents discussing the October, 1962, Cuban Missile Crisis. I certainly did not understand all the complexities of this scary political event, but I remember that my parents were very alarmed and scared when listening to the national news on our square RCA black and white TV set. Dad said to Mom, "Do you really think they are crazy enough to shoot missiles off down there?" That got my attention, what in the heck were "missiles," and where is "down there?" Thankfully, our young President Kennedy resolved this serious crisis in a peaceful manner when using his "flexible response" military strategy that included naval/air blockades and negotiating from a position of strength when dealing with the evil Communist dictators, Soviet Premier Khrushchev and Cuban revolutionary fanatic Fidel Castro.

But the event that I remember most vividly that really had a dramatic impact upon my childhood was the tragic assassination of President Kennedy on November 22, 1963. It was a cold Friday afternoon in North Little Rock, Arkansas, and my older brother and I were walking home from our neighborhood school (pre-integration days in the South.) I was in the first grade and my brother was in the third grade. We lived only a block away from school, and back then most kids walked back and forth to school. There were literally no big yellow school buses around in those days. As we approached our home at about 3:30 p.m. Central Time, our next-door neighbor Billy stuck his head out of his front door and shouted, "The president has been shot! The president has been shot! Turn on your TV!"

We were, of course, shocked by this news. We knew it was tragic, but at that tender age we did   not realize the full gravity of the situation. Our neighbor, Kermit, who lived across the street from us, was home at the time and she directed us and several other kids to come in and listen to the news on her TV. She wisely told us kids that this was very tragic and historic news, and that we needed to be quiet and listen carefully.

Shortly afterward, we heard those now-famous words from CBS news anchor Walter Cronkite   on live black and white TV. Cronkite paused and slowly took his black horn-rimmed glasses off, cleared his throat and, with a tear rolling down his wrinkled face, he said, "We have now confirmed, the President of the United States is dead." In contrast, a youthful-looking CBS anchor named Dan Rather was also visibly shaken by the tragedy, but he then spoke more about the horrible details that occurred that dark day in downtown Dallas, Texas, including how Texas Governor Conley was also shot but survived death. Vice President Lyndon B. Johnson and First Lady Jackie Kennedy were also with the president that day but were not injured. Shortly after President Kennedy's death, VP Johnson, his wife Mrs. "Ladybird" Johnson, and First Lady Jacqueline Kennedy reboarded Air Force One and headed back to Washington, DC. Before the plane took off, VP Johnson was sworn in as the new US president, with Jackie Kennedy tearfully standing by his side still in her blood-stained pink dress suit.

She left her red-stained suit on until she arrived back at the White House because she wanted to "show   the world" what "they" did to her husband. The young radical Lee Harvey Oswald was promptly arrested for the shootings by Dallas police but was shot and killed two days later by local night club owner Jack Ruby – on live TV! The technical details and motives of these crazy events have   been investigated for many years, and the conclusions remain controversial to this day.

On Monday, November 25, 1963, President Kennedy was laid to rest at Arlington National Cemetery in Washington DC with full military honors, including a horse-drawn casket and a 21-gun salute. Many world leaders, members of Congress, and other dignitaries attended this very sad event that was broadcasted on national TV. Newly sworn-in President Johnson declared that Monday as a National Day of Mourning. All the schools and many offices around the country were closed in honor of our slain president. I will never forget watching this sad historic event with my mother that day, the images of the young Kennedy family dressed in black, marching beside the horse-drawn casket, all the military honors and fancy uniforms on display. But the most memorable image for my six-year-old mind to absorb was when the Kennedy brothers lit the now famous "eternal flame" by President Kennedy's grave, which was fueled by a newly installed natural gas line, the symbol of eternal life and justice for all. My sweet, compassionate, conservative mother began to cry because she was so moved by this final gesture. I then asked my mom, "Why are you crying? Didn't you and Daddy vote for the other man?" She responded in her soft voice: "Yes, honey, we voted for the other candidate, but none of that matters today. The father of our country is dead, and this is a very sad day for all of us. Today, we are all just Americans."

After I heard those profound words from my mom, I suddenly understood the full gravity of this tragic event. Even at the tender age of six, this sparked my interest in news and politics, and I started to understand that there was more to life than playing baseball and watching Saturday morning cartoons with my brothers. I understood that this world could be very violent when people disagree about things. I also understood that violence was not a good way to solve problems.

Throughout my grade school years, the events of the 1960s got crazier. Soon, the nightly TV news broadcasts centered around the buildup of the war in Vietnam, civil rights protests, and the exciting space race. Again, I didn't understand all the complex social and political details at the time, but our parents encouraged us to listen and learn from these global and national current events. We now know that the Vietnam War was very mismanaged during the Cold War era, and I remember watching the live TV announcement by President Johnson on March 31, 1968, that he had decided not to run for re-election. My parents' mouths dropped wide open in shock, but they were relieved that we would be having new leadership the next year, hopefully giving Nixon another shot at the White House, which he won decisively in November, 1968, running against Vice President Hubert Humphrey. President Johnson had a lot of success with domestic legislation, most notably the landmark 1964 Civil Rights Act and the 1965 Voting Rights Act. Civil rights leader Martin Luther King, Jr., was at the peak of his influence then. He knew that he needed the support of many moderate

Republicans in Congress to get these bills passed into law, while many southern Democrats voted against these historic reforms. We also now know that many of Johnson's well-intended "Great Society" and "War on Poverty" programs have been a long-term failure for the same basic reasons: they were too complex and expensive, especially while financing the escalating Vietnam War and space programs and, most importantly, they encouraged a long-term dependence on government handouts instead of providing short-term relief for needy citizens. In other words, even with the noblest intentions, the "welfare culture" that started in the 1960s has been an overall tragedy for America. This long-term government dependence has eroded traditional family values. It has discouraged career training/education and it has reduced the basic work ethic that made America the envy of the world.

During the late 1960s I became somewhat more news savvy by watching Sunday morning programs such as "Meet the Press" when TV reporters were much fairer and more balanced when questioning the leaders of our country, and by reading more details of current events in the newspaper , which was also more objective at the time.

More violent tragedies rocked our country in 1968. Martin Luther King, Jr., was assassinated on April 4 at a Memphis hotel while standing beside his young assistant Rev. Jesse Jackson. I remember so well that my widowed grandmother Mamie phoned us long distance from her nearby home in Memphis because she was alarmed and frightened from the violent rioting that had begun from angry followers of Dr. King. She could hear the noise of the crowds from her front porch and was afraid that the violence would spread across the town and into her neighborhood that night.

In June of 1968, Robert Kennedy was shot and killed in Los Angeles right after he won the Democratic presidential primary. The gory details were captured by TV cameras while he laid in a pool of blood inside the hotel kitchen. All Americans were horrified that another tragedy had stricken the Kennedy family.

The 1968 third-party presidential candidate, George Wallace, former Governor of Alabama who carried five southern states, would be shot in 1972. He survived the shooting, but it left him paralyzed for the rest of his life.

These shocking events wore on my young mind, and intensified my belief that all this violence was destroying our country.

On a more positive note, the 1960s' space race was a very exciting time for grade school kids. At that same caring neighborhood school that was only a block away from home, our teachers made a point to bring TV sets to our classrooms to watch the launch of the big space rockets. It was so cool to watch these events live because anything could have happened – sometimes NASA had to postpone the actual launch for various reasons, usually due to a minor technical glitch, but the delays were usually short. We often had a science lesson based around these rocket launches which made them even more meaningful.

My favorite TV announcer while watching space news events was always Walter Cronkite because he really studied and enjoyed the technical details, and he reminded the audience that the late President Kennedy set the national goal of landing men on the moon by the end of the decade. Every one of these space missions during the '60s were really just another small step toward that ambitious goal: to win the space race before the Soviet Union.

That breath-taking goal was achieved on July 20, 1969, the summer after I completed the sixth grade. I will never forget watching that magical moment with the entire family that evening in our living room. We had already heard those famous words, "Houston, the Eagle has landed," when the small moon capsule first landed on the moon surface, but now Neil Armstrong and Buzz Aldrin were about to actually WALK on the moon! As Armstrong began walking down those ladder steps, the TV cameras came on, and nobody really knew if we would be able to see the TV images from Earth – but it worked beautifully! My greatest-generation parents were in awe to be witnessing this live historic event. I remember my Dad saying, with his eyes tearing up: "Mama, can you believe what we are seeing on TV? I never thought we would live long enough to see a man walking on the moon. This is a miracle."

After the two brave Americans made it out from the capsule and planted an American flag, with wires to make it appear to be waving, President Nixon spoke to them and congratulated them – on live TV for the nation to hear. We were all relieved when our brave astronauts made it back safely to earth. They were given a hero's welcome and became national celebrities.

Shortly after the first manned moon landing, the next big cultural event that I remember was the huge outdoor rock festival that took place in upstate New York called "Woodstock." This event was a wild and crazy rock-n-roll festival that lasted several days. Thousands of young people attended. This event included a lot of "anti-establishment" behavior that reinforced the '60s hippie image of "sex, drugs, and rock-n-roll." The original organizers of Woodstock have admitted that they grossly underestimated the huge audience turnout and the related problems that ensued. During the festival, rain created a muddy outdoor mess but most of the young folks that attended just had fun while the biggest rock stars of the day such as Janice Joplin, Jimi Hendrix, and Carlos Santana kept on performing.

This historic event also inspired many of the anti-Vietnam War protests throughout the country, especially on college campuses, as more young people were dying in a war that many believed could not be won. As these anti-war protests were being covered more by the mainstream media, I started to read and study more about the foreign policies of our federal government. The more I learned, the more I agreed that the Vietnam War was not only a mistake, it was grossly mismanaged. As I started junior high school in the fall of 1969, this viewpoint only worsened, especially when hearing stories about local young men that were either wounded or killed in the jungles of Vietnam. The overall goal of the Vietnam War was to "stop the spread of communism," which was proven to be an utter failure in the spring of 1975 when I was about to graduate high school. I will always remember those TV images of the North Vietnam communist army capturing the South Vietnam capitol that ended the war in shameful defeat. Over 50,000 young Americans were killed for a lost cause, not to mention the many seriously wounded and the tax dollars that were wasted. Failed national leadership is very expensive indeed. Even with all the failures of Vietnam and social unrest of the '60s, most people I knew back then were more patriotic, more family-oriented (including minority groups), harder-working, more loyal and honest, and kinder than today.

I cannot ever remember a PERFECT America,

but I do remember a BETTER America!

CHAPTER 3

The Serious 1970s

As I now reflect on those crazy social and political events from a "young" senior citizen perspective, I also remember many positive and heart-warming efforts from parents, teachers, coaches, and even strangers. While young adults were fighting in Vietnam and many African Americans were still fighting for their basic civil rights, by some miracle we kids were also having a lot of wholesome fun.

I now realize that most of our adult mentors at the time sheltered us kids back then from the horrors of war and urban violence. Yes, they knew we baby boomers were basically the "first TV generation" that had regular access to the daily news, but my compassionate teachers and coaches never dwelled on the "bad news" – they made a point to stay positive and to provide constant learning activities that were both fun and practical. They stressed that hard work, patriotism, and following the accepted rules of society would usually lead to success and happiness. Friendly competition and good sportsmanship were the rule of the day, and there was no such thing as "participation awards" – you played to win, you aspired for excellence the "American way." Teachers, parents, and coaches were almost always on the same page – they were not enemies competing for your approval, rather they were united allies, dedicated to your success.

For example, during that wild and crazy "summer of love" of 1969, my brothers and I were having a blast playing on championship baseball teams at our beloved local Burns Park in North Little Rock. Our long-time baseball coach, Mr. Williams, had a profound positive impact upon my young life, and he was like a second father to me. He worked as a local police officer and spent many, many hours working with us kids in the Arkansas heat on a volunteer basis, and his two sons also played on the same team. Coach Williams was tough on us during our teeny and little league years; we were either playing a formal league game in our sharp-looking green and white uniforms, or we were practicing for several hours out in the hot summer heat. Some parents thought he was a bit rough around the edges - after all, we were still "just kids," right? "Coach" was also a military veteran and played several years in both the minor and major leagues in the Pittsburg Pirates organization. This man knew baseball inside and out and he was always in teaching mode – he was clearly the best coach in our league. During those crazy '60s we won five straight district championships, and in August, 1969, we won the overall state championship. In other words, we were literally the BEST little league baseball team in the entire state of Arkansas that year. We were the best because Mr. Williams taught us very valuable life lessons at an early age. Yes, we were fundamentally good athletes, but Coach maintained very high standards. He taught us that whatever you decide to do in life, nothing replaces hard work, discipline, and dedication. Our parents also had great respect for his leadership. They did not always agree with his decisions and tough demeanor, but they told us kids that we needed to respect his authority because "he was the boss."

After games, Coach also hosted team picnics and swim parties that demonstrated his softer side. All the families would contribute and bring homemade southern favorites such as fried chicken, home-grown Arkansas tomatoes, potato salad, fresh sweet iced tea with lemons, and strawberry shortcake. Before leaving, he always told us that he was very proud of us because we were all "winners" - we were all part of the "team" - we were an extension of his family. This winning and compassionate attitude has instilled confidence within me my entire life. I was so lucky to have this positive male role model during those challenging times.

My teachers and coaches at school modeled similar positive professional behavior, and most parents followed their advice and volunteered regularly to help with wholesome school activities. Halloween carnivals were so much fun and raised needed money for school functions. Parents would donate used items for rummage sales (mini flea markets), and homemade pies and candy for bake sales.

Parents would volunteer to sell soft drinks, popcorn, and cotton candy.... or donate their time to work at the spook house or the go-fishing booth. They would also help teachers with activities such as paper drives, school plays, Valentine dances, and occasional "Coca-Cola and cookie" parties to reward good behavior.

My football coaches were also on the "tough side" compared to today's standards, but our parents instructed us baby boomers to respect their authority and follow the rules. As student athletes we did not always agree with their instructions, but we obeyed their decisions because they were the authority figures.

I remember distinctly my junior high principal gave a brief talk in the football locker room at the beginning of summer practice in the early '70s. His message was brief and straight-forward. He stated, "Young men, I admire all of you for giving up some of your summer vacation to practice football for our team this year, especially in this heat; but, let me remind you that the coaches are in charge - they are the bosses of this football program. None of you are required to participate. This is a volunteer school activity. You have all chosen to be a part of this team. If you disagree with the coaches, don't waste your time complaining to me – you are free to leave the team at any time. But, if you decide to stick with it - and I hope you will - I expect all of you to follow the rules, obey your coaches, and play to win!"

During my years in junior high school, current events were not improving much. The war in Vietnam continued to drag on throughout Nixon's first term in office, and anti-war protests became larger and even more vocal as Americans watched the daily casualty numbers increase on the evening news.

Even though candidate Nixon promised to end the war, he quickly realized that he inherited a very complex and "hot war" stalemate from the Johnson administration. The media began to describe this bloody mess as the "big muddy." They also began to broadcast very graphic war documentaries on prime-time TV during the early '70s that were real eye-openers, especially for young people and parents that had loved ones over in those far-away jungles. People from all sides of the political spectrum were becoming more and more frustrated every day and were demanding different actions from our government. Conservatives were shouting, "Do what it takes to win the war - we are the most powerful nation in the world!" Liberals were loudly protesting a simple recommendation to "end the war now!" President Nixon continued to pledge that he would end the war, but he stated that his administration would only support "peace with honor" that coincided with the original mission of stopping the spread of communism. He did order gradual American troop withdrawals during this period, but young soldiers were still dying every day, and many citizens lost complete faith in   the overall mission.

I remember well when my older brother told me about a classmate of his who was called to the front school office one day in the spring of 1970 to receive a tragic message from his family. They informed the classmate that his older brother was just killed during combat in Vietnam. We never actually knew personally this slain young American, but my brother and I began to understand the pain and suffering of war when this young life was lost from our own hometown. From our teenage perspective, it appeared there was no end in sight, and every year we became closer to the drafting age of 18.

Finally, one evening in late January, 1973, a peace agreement to end America's war involvement in Vietnam was announced! I happened to be working at the local pizza parlor when the manager announced this historic news over the same PA system that we used for the pizza pickup procedure. The   restaurant was already just about at capacity and the customers went nuts with jubilation! People were cheering and shouting, "It's over, at last! Thank God this damn war is over!" The bar area began to get crowded. Folks were buying large pitchers of beer to celebrate, the piano player started new tunes, and people were dancing, even though it was against the local ordinance at the time. This scene of celebration was right out of a movie. It left a memorable impression upon my young mind, and I thought to myself (correctly) that this day would certainly be documented in future history books.

Even though Americans were relieved that the Vietnam War was about over, the daily news focus quickly shifted to many other domestic issues. The continued space manned missions to the moon now included a new cool "moon rover" that was like a motorized go-cart that explored expanded regions of the moon's surface. The ongoing struggle of civil rights for minority groups and women, and environmental and consumer protection movements were also main stories of the day.

When I was in the eighth grade, forced public school racial integration via mass busing was very controversial. Most people I knew in central Arkansas supported equal rights, but a lot of folks on both sides were opposed to mass busing because they believed this program was too abrupt and too expensive, while also restricting freedoms of "school choice" and "local control of schools." President Nixon and Congress pushed forward with these federal mandates in the name of constitutional civil rights, similar to Eisenhower's order during the 1957 Little Rock Central High crisis.

I remember how strange and different it was to watch kids from across town being bused in that year, and sincerely thought that it was an unfair hardship for those families. However, we were still teenagers and adapted in short order. There were a few racially motivated scuffles and disagreements during my junior high years that virtually disappeared later in high school. My teachers and coaches again rose to the occasion and kept their promise to treat every student fairly, regardless of their background or zip code. This was the same time period that I first heard that famous saying, "It's not where you are from, it's where you are going that matters," from my coaches.

Then came more American political drama…Watergate! President Nixon was in his second term in office, and had managed to get major domestic reforms through a Democrat-controlled Congress by accepting compromises, and by maintaining a spirit for trying new ideas to solve common problems. He was very "progressive" compared to today's

Republican leaders. The Watergate scandal was complex and very draining for the American people. It involved several key members of the Nixon administration and staff members of the 1972 Committee to Re-elect the President and, of course, President Nixon himself.

The main crime committed by President Nixon was actually the "cover-up" of the break-in burglary of the Democrat headquarters during the 1972 campaign season. He always stated that he never ordered the break-in by overzealous campaign staff members, but later it was proven that he was involved in the cover-up and lied to the American people. When he learned that Congress had the votes to not only impeach, but to convict and remove him from office, he was forced to resign on August 9, 1974. Vice President Gerald Ford then became our new president. It was another sad time for our country to witness, especially for conservatives. During my high school years I remember that "Nixon" and "Watergate" became dirty words, and young people, especially, became very cynical about government leadership, even on a state and local level. Many people, including myself, considered that the real tragedy of Watergate was that it overshadowed all the positive achievements of Richard Nixon over   those many years of public service, and that it had destroyed the morale of the American people, at least in the short term. The real lesson we learned from the Watergate scandal was that no one in America should be above the law, even the president of the United Sates. Shortly after taking office, President Ford made the controversial decision to grant Nixon a full pardon for "all crimes, present and future." It was a very unpopular decision because many citizens thought that Nixon should have been punished more severely for his sins in office. I remember watching the TV news clip of President Ford that evening and thinking to myself that the Democrats will beat him over the head with this speech down the road, which they did during the 1976 election. President Ford argued that Nixon and the country had suffered enough, and that this pardon was the only way to close this tragic chapter of history and move on to solve more pressing national problems such as rising inflation, unemployment, and gas shortages.

As I walked through my high school graduation line in the spring of 1975, President Ford was becoming increasingly unpopular. America formally lost the Vietnam War in April of 1975 as I watched the last surge of the Communist North

Vietnam army conquer the capitol of South Vietnam. It was a painful reminder of a long and mismanaged war that really accomplished nothing for our   country.

I remember that President Ford came out with "WIN" buttons that stood for "Whip Inflation Now." This noble attempt to motivate Americans to support reduced federal spending, thereby   reducing national inflation, went over like a lead balloon. The public and media viewed it as "political spin" and over-simplistic. All these domestic problems that were still fresh in Americans' minds, were probably the main reason former Georgia Governor Jimmy Carter won the 1976 presidential election.

I was now in my second year of college, and surrounded by young liberal Democrats that loved the new optimism that a Carter presidency might provide. At the time, even I thought he was really cool and sharp, and thought he would perform well in the White House. I remember well the newspaper headlines the day after he took office: "President Carter Promises New Hope for the Old Dream," alluding to, of course, the famous "American Dream." Throughout my undergraduate college years at the University of Central Arkansas during the late 1970s, I followed the news more intensely, sometimes for class assignments. As the Carter years transpired, I became very disappointed with President Carter's leadership performance and the general direction of our country. Inflation and interest rates reached out-of-control "double-digit" percentages, and unemployment also remained too high. In 1979, a foreign affairs disaster hit the Carter White House. Our American embassy in Tehran, Iran, was captured by "student radicals," and a large group of our diplomats became political hostages, which outraged Americans. I will never forget those disturbing TV images of our diplomats, blindfolded and tied up, being dragged out like animals to be displayed for the world to witness.

This crisis dragged on through the 1980 presidential election and was a major reason former California Governor Ronald Reagan defeated Carter by a landslide decision. The American public were sick and tired of domestic economic and foreign policy failures. Reagan represented a new strength and confidence that America needed, and later the new President Reagan indeed delivered on those promises.

After I graduated from college in the summer of 1980, I became more astute regarding historical, political, and social events. No, I surely did not have all the answers just because I was a new college graduate, but I did learn to study and research current events, trends, and policies from a more objective perspective. I now relied more on documented facts and figures, and less on emotions and images, to make my young adult decisions.

I cannot ever remember a PERFECT America,

but I do remember a BETTER America!

CHAPTER 4

The Roaring 1980s

The night of the historic Reagan presidential landslide in November, 1980, I was working hard in the back room at the grocery clerk job that got me through high school and college. Now in my seventh year of hard blue-collar night shifts, I was ready for a change as a new college graduate. My degree was in business administration and marketing, and I was in the process of interviewing for a professional white-collar sales career. As a young and idealistic college-educated man, I still basically liked Jimmy Carter and believed he maintained the noble goals of peace, especially in the Middle East after he brokered the Camp David Accords in 1978, and international social/economic justice. But, I knew in my heart that his domestic economic policies were simply not working, and the 1979/80 Iranian Hostage Crisis situation was unacceptable, including the failed military rescue attempt.

I remember well when a co-worker entered our backroom work area about 8:30 p.m. that evening and told us that Reagan was "running away with it," and was beating President Carter "like a drum." My work buddies and I were somewhat shocked that it was becoming a landslide victory for Reagan, but I did feel a sense of relief that major changes were soon on the way.

The early '80s were still a very tough time for many Americans, especially young people that were just starting their careers. After the failed economic policies of the Carter administration, the inflation rate and prime interest rates were still in the double-digits, and unemployment rates remained high across the country, especially in once-thriving industrial areas. The lingering negative effects of the '70s' energy crisis and the federal over-spending for the Vietnam War, space race, and ongoing social programs of Johnson's "Great Society" administration had taken their collective toll on the country.

The professional job market for young college graduates in central Arkansas was especially tight, and the increased hiring enforcement of the federal "affirmative action" programs created in the mid-'60s made this already tight job market especially competitive for me as a male Caucasian. There were still decent career opportunities available to me, but the better ones required long-term site relocation to other larger cities such as Dallas, Tulsa, Memphis, St. Louis, etc. I was newly engaged to my college girlfriend who had just accepted her first "career job" locally, and I thought an out-of-state transfer was not practical at the time. Most of these interviews for my first career job transpired during Reagan's presidential transition period, and the more I learned about his plans to revive the economy and regain our military strength, the more I agreed with this conservative philosophy of cutting taxes and reducing government regulations.

The day that I really began considering myself a "conservative" came after one of my job interviews. A very nice and mature human resources manager from a national company blew my young mind one day with his blunt honesty. He said, "Well, young man, you have the exact educational and work experience background that we are looking for. I liked all of your responses and references, and I think you would be an excellent employee for our company.... but I can't hire you now." I responded, "Well, thank you for the kind words, but why can't you hire me now? I would love to be a part of your team." He stated, "Are you familiar with 'affirmative action' programs? My company has recently adhered to federal guidelines that strongly encourage us to hire a specific number of female and minority job candidates, even if their qualifications are less than male and Caucasian candidates. I appreciate your time, maybe we will have a 'slot' for you that matches your demographic some time down the road."

To say that I was disappointed to hear these words would be an understatement! I literally could not believe that a professional HR Director was saying this to me. This was a classic example of "hiring quotas" of specific demographic groups created by a federal policy called "affirmative action." In my opinion, this program is nothing short of reverse discrimination. Once again, even with the noble goal of ensuring equal employment opportunities for all citizens, this '60s' federal program was over-zealous and misguided, especially with their program implementation and enforcement.

In late January, 1981, President Reagan was sworn into office in grand style, wearing a formal tux with tails and with the new glamourous First Lady Nancy Reagan by his side. The former California   Governor and Hollywood B-movie actor quickly won the hearts of most Americans, and he signed new executive orders to start his federal budget cuts the first day in office. My family loved him and agreed with his "supply-side" economic policies of increasing production, cutting personal taxes 25% over the first three years, reducing regulations but increasing the defense budget to rebuild the military and win the Cold War.

I remember watching the inauguration with my parents and grandmother. The country was still in a deep recession and people were hungry for a new direction in leadership. My Grandma Mamie called Reagan "a REAL man," and my mother was excited that he started the federal budget-cutting the very first day. She said, "That-a-boy, Ronnie! Get that budget-cutting knife out and don't stop!" Another huge development that first day of the Reagan era was that the Iranian hostages were finally released unharmed after about a year and half, and the country was relieved that nightmare was over. The now-former President Carter made the public announcement late that day and basically took credit for their healthy release–- but most people that I knew gave Reagan the credit, and theorized that the Iranians were scared of the new tough and strong image of President Reagan.

America was anxious for a new beginning in the early '80s, and they were basically supportive of President Reagan's first actions. Taxes were indeed cut, regulations started to decrease, and major budget cuts began to be implemented mainly within federal social and environmental programs.

Reagan regularly presented a stronger and more confident TV image than Carter, while maintaining a great sense of humor, even with a hostile White House press core led by ABC TV reporter Sam Donaldson. Early in his first year in the spring of 1981, Reagan and his press secretary James Brady were both shot with 22 caliber bullets by a mentally ill critic, John Hinckley. They both survived, but Brady was left permanently brain damaged that day at the Washington DC Hilton hotel. I attended a national convention at this same location as a young city councilman in March, 1990, and toured the exact site of these tragic shootings. While I was standing at this same spot, it instantly brought back the TV video clip images we watched that evening in 1981, of Mr. Brady on the ground receiving first aid, the president being shoved into the presidential "beast" limo, and the brave secret service agent that literally "took a bullet" for the new president. Thankfully, President Reagan made a swift recovery and returned to full-time duty at the White House only after about two weeks. This event only increased his popularity and "tough" image. Brady's serious misfortune created a new debate about national gun control legislation and, indeed, the future "Brady Gun Control Bill" was named in his honor.

Due to Reagan's conservative economic policies, America finally started to recover from the deep recession in 1983, and the long-term recovery was in full swing going into the 1984 re-election campaign.

One of the most exciting events of my life was in October, 1984, when my younger brother and I were able to see and hear President Reagan speak in person at a downtown Little Rock hotel. The Arkansas Republican party was giving away free limited printed tickets, but you had to get registered and in the security screening line at least two hours in advance on a Saturday morning. We were both now official "Reagan Republican Conservatives" because we were now convinced that his first-term agenda policies had worked for the whole country. We were both recently married with young sons, gainfully employed and doing pretty well for ourselves. While we were certainly not getting rich, we now believed we had a bright future ahead of us and we were convinced that America was heading in the right direction. We agreed with Reagan's now famous re-election theme "IT'S MORNING AGAIN IN AMERICA!" symbolizing a renewed optimism in the country.

We were standing about ten rows from the president with an excellent center view. He was bigger than life back then, truly a surreal moment for us. His campaign stump speech in 1984 centered on his tax cuts and keeping his promise to cut bureaucratic red tape and rebuild our military. He never mentioned that this combination of policy reforms also ballooned the national deficit, but I don't think anyone attending that rally really cared about the deficit that day, they believed that America was back and President Ronald Reagan was the reason why! That next month President Reagan won a huge landslide re-election victory over former VP Walter Mondale, cementing his popular mandate for a second term in office.

Shortly after Reagan was celebrating his second term in office, most Americans had a renewed confidence in the overall improvements of the national economy. Inflation and interest rates were greatly reduced and stabilized, new decent-paying jobs were created because major corporations were expanding and hiring again. Our national defenses were being bolstered to maintain peace and security.

My younger brother and I shared this feeling of optimism and confidence when we started two local service businesses from scratch in the spring of 1985. With a little bit of money and a lot of hope and hard work, we started a lawn mowing/trimming service during the spring and summer months, and a chimney sweep/fireplace repair service mainly during the fall and winter months. We serviced a lot of the same clients for both of these common needs in primarily middle-class neighborhoods, and met many very nice people who appreciated our simple honesty and work ethic. We were blessed to quickly receive a lot of repeat business and client referrals based on this simple business plan in the central Arkansas market. Again, we were not getting rich, but just having this initial success and the freedom of running our own businesses at this young age was very exciting and rewarding, and renewed our faith in the "American Dream!"

Early in 1986, a major scandal rocked the Reagan administration. A news leak revealed that officials had negotiated an "arms-for-hostages" deal with the radical government of Iran. This scandal was complex and contained a lot of moving parts involving the CIA and our military that were hard to follow for most Americans, but the bottom line was that it was a complete contradiction of Reagan's hard line against the "outlaw state" of Iran, a country that supported acts of terrorism. This scandal was known as the "Iran-Contra Affair," and it was heavily criticized by the mass media, Democrats, and even some conservative Republicans who thought this policy contradiction hurt the creditability of Reagan and the entire Republican Party. In my opinion, this scandal was probably Reagan's worst leadership mistake of his entire time in office, and the most difficult event to explain to the American people, to say the least. However, it appeared that shortly after all the messy details were disclosed, including detailed televised congressional hearings that were very critical of Marine Lt. Colonel Oliver North's leadership decisions, most folks just moved on with their lives as normal. The Reagan charm prevailed once again.

I remember watching the Sunday morning news program commentators (mostly liberal) during this time air their anger and frustration about how "President Reagan is off the hook again, nothing negative ever appears to stick to him, the man is just TEFLON" (referring to the smooth surface used for "stick-free" cooking.)

I became actively involved in my first local political campaign in the spring of 1986, when a dear neighborhood friend asked me to help him with his city council race. He was still young and active in community affairs, college-educated, honest, and a devout Catholic. We ran a solid, positive campaign on a shoe-string budget against a popular older incumbent, and we lost by a small margin. We accepted defeat graciously and chalked it up to experience, but that was when I was bitten by the political bug and started to get more involved with local affairs in my beloved hometown of North Little Rock.

In the spring of 1988, I decided to run for city councilman in that same ward, again on a shoe-string budget, but with new experience and a base of support of mainly old school and church friends. Back then, in central Arkansas, the Democrat Party ruled, and most candidates did not have any realistic chance of winning if you did not run in the spring Democrat primary, even in local races. By then I certainly considered myself a conservative Republican, but I was surrounded by moderate southern

Democrats who were very traditional, and they supported keeping the Democrat Party dominant. As an eager 30-year-old former athlete who played to win, I went ahead and filed as a Democrat for the March 1988 "Super Tuesday" primary. After a lot of hard work and old-fashioned door-to-door campaigning (pre-internet/social media days), I was blessed to garner enough votes to be leading in a run-off and, after more hard work, two weeks later we won the run-off. I was so happy and humbled because I knew the only way we won was from the hard work of friends and volunteers, especially from my family. Later that summer, an older gentleman that I did not know from my ward announced he was running as an Independent, which forced us to run a third race. We repeated the winning process to capture that city council seat, effective January 1, 1989.

The fall of 1988 was an exciting time for me. I really felt that I was now entering "mature adulthood." I also felt very lucky, again, to have the privilege of working my own local businesses, and now the very unique opportunity of serving as an elected official! My family and friends continued to be supportive while I served in this new capacity and I enjoyed working with new friends and rewarding projects, especially those helping my constituents to solve old problems.

The Reagan administration was winding down and Vice President George (H.W.) Bush was now running to be president. Bush reminded Americans every day about the "peace and prosperity" of the Reagan years, especially the greatly improved economy and a much stronger military. But, most historians agree that the greatest achievements of the Reagan years were probably winning the Cold War over the Soviet Union, the collapse of communism in Eastern Europe, and the many conservative appointments he made to the judicial branch of government. President Reagan appointed 368 new federal judges and three new Supreme Court judges, including Antonin Scalia, Anthony Kennedy, and, the first female to the court, Sandra Day O'Conner. Even though Reagan failed to decrease the overall size and scope of the huge federal government, the Cold War was probably won by his support of the expensive MX missile system and the high tech SDI (Strategic Defense Initiative), commonly known as "Star Wars." He knew that the Soviets could not compete with these systems without collapsing their economy.

Another very exciting historical moment my younger brother and I experienced was on October 27, 1988, at the Little Rock airport. President Reagan came back to Little Rock on Air Force One on short notice to personally campaign for VP Bush and other state Republicans. It was another huge turnout of several thousand people because Reagan and Bush remained very popular in our neck of the woods. We again had a location close to the speaking stage because we knew to arrive early for the security screening. Local singing artist and devout conservative Terry Rose served as the Master of Ceremonies. He was receiving audio updates of the president's flight arrival and passing on the info to the large anxious crowd. Mr. Rose became a local folk legend when he recorded his popular holiday   hit song "Christmastime in Arkansas Again", which epitomizes the traditional Christian values of most people in Arkansas, especially conservative Republicans.

After waiting for almost two hours, the big, beautiful, blue and white Air Force One came swooping down to land, then slowly inched toward the stage. In a few more minutes, we could see the military brass coming down the plane steps with the famous "nuclear football" case handcuffed to his wrist. Then, President Reagan came out of the plane, waving to the crowd, looking a bit older than he did in 1984, but still with that movie star smile, and making his way to the stage….the crowd went wild! The president then leaned into the microphone and told the crowd that the winning Arkansas Razorbacks and UCA Bears football teams were "his kind of teams," warming up the excited crowd. Then   the more formal campaign speech began: "Well, today I've come to Little Rock for a very special reason. I want to talk to you about a friend of mine, the next president of the United States, George Bush." The crowd started clapping loudly and several people shouted "We love you, Mr. President!" He continued with a "vintage Reagan" stump speech that summarized the achievements of the last eight years, and asked the crowd again to make VP Bush "President Bush" on November 8th.

At the end, the popular Arkansas Republican Congressman John Paul Hammerschmidt handed the president a red sign that said "I'm a 'BUSH' HOG," alluding to the Arkansas Razorback mascot. The large crowd started singing a local folk tune: "Oh, Arkansas, Oh, Arkansas, Arkansas USA!" about a dozen times, and the President of the United States joined in with that big smile of his! This image was memorable and, with chill bumps running up my spine, I was very proud to be an American that day and equally proud to be an Arkansan!

On November 8, 1988, VP Bush indeed became President-elect Bush, by soundly defeating liberal Democrat Massachusetts Governor Mike Dukakis, winning 38 states.

Bush had a much different background than Reagan, and governed the next few years in a more moderate and compromising style. His tenure as president coincided exactly with the years that I served as an elected city councilman in North Little Rock.

In the spring of 1992, I again had the privilege to see and hear another president "up close, in person" at a convention in Washington DC which will be discussed in the next chapter.

I cannot ever remember a PERFECT America,

but I do remember a BETTER America!

CHAPTER 5

The Go-Go 1990s

At about noon on January 1, 1989, I took the oath of office to serve as the youngest member of   the North Little Rock City Council. Now age 31, I was very proud and happy that day to place my left hand on the Holy Bible with my family standing by me and promise to serve to the best of my ability. That same day at City Hall, two other new aldermen and a new mayor were also sworn into   office.

The early March 1988, "Super Tuesday" election cycle that year created a long and unhealthy "lame duck" period. We were all running against the incumbents because of several of their unpopular decisions; therefore, it was practically a clean sweep victory for us. Our new Mayor was a popular local attorney and state representative who also possessed a cool name that was perfect for politics: Patrick Henry Hays. Mayor Pat had a huge positive influence on my young life. He was about ten years older than I and more politically savvy. He was always cordial and loved to help people. Unlike myself, he considered himself a "centrist Democrat," and was a huge Bill and Hillary Clinton fan, whereas I, on the other hand, still strongly supported the more conservative Reagan-Bush agenda even though I realized that they were not perfect, either. I was still disappointed that Reagan had not been able to reduce our federal debt after eight years.

Soon afterward, on January 20, 1989, George Herbert Walker Bush was sworn in as our 41st president. My family and I were delighted that Vice President Bush was now our new president to continue the conservative Reagan agenda, but we soon learned that Bush would govern differently. During the 1988 campaign, Bush famously promised, "Read my lips, NO NEW TAXES!" in a stern and confident tone. These words would later come back to haunt him at re-election time. These were still basically considered good times in America. The inflation and unemployment rates were stable at around 5%, and interest rates were about half of what they were at the end of Carter's term. I built and financed my first new house in 1989 and was happy to finance it at a flat 10% that year.

Because Bush had more of a professional background and interest in foreign affairs, and because Democrats maintained majority control in Congress, the new Bush administration did not propose many new domestic proposals. The president vetoed newly passed bills expanding worker discrimination and family medical leave rights, but supported the new ADA legislation (Americans with Disabilities Act) that many conservatives and businesspeople considered too broad and expensive. I remember right after this new law became enacted many of my city council and mayor peers around the state were upset because, while they supported the civil rights of the handicapped, they were concerned that the costs were too high for most cities to absorb on their own. Congress and the federal government back then had developed a very bad habit called "unfunded mandates." These popular social programs would easily win the support from most voters, but the Feds would just mandate the complex and expensive rules/regulations down to state and local governments, and then would refuse to actually fund these new programs. Therefore, I quickly learned that these federal practices were creating a new massive problem for local governments, namely forcing them to find new ways to fund these mandates. In other words, CREATE NEW LOCAL TAXES! As a young conservative, that new reality really upset me and, of course, most of my middle-class hard-working constituents did not approve of ANY new local fees and/or taxes! Our first couple of years in local office were tough. The city started to have major budget problems. Federal "revenue-sharing" funds were drying up, heavy equipment was aging, and expensive new monthly bond debt payments for a voter-approved hydro-electric dam plant were starting. We called two different special tax elections in 1989 and 1990 to raise needed revenue, and they were both soundly defeated by the public. In essence, our people told us "Read our lips! No new taxes!"

In August, 1990, the unfortunate winds of war were beginning to blow again when Iraq's ruthless dictator Saddam Hussein decided to invade their oil-rich neighbor Kuwait. President Bush took swift and decisive action against this totally unjustified military aggression. He used his previous United Nations (UN) experience to successfully lead resolutions condemning these actions. He demanded a total withdrawal from

Kuwait and imposed trade/economic sanctions. After Hussein's arrogant refusal, Bush then successfully led new UN resolutions demanding withdrawal by January 15, 1991, or face military action by a broad American-led coalition, and even garnered Congressional approval for war actions against Iraq. The "Butcher of Bagdad" still refused to withdraw his troops from Kuwait by the transparent deadline, and President Bush ordered the full force of the American military to be unleashed upon Iraq. Through massive American air strikes and a swift ground operation, the first Persian Gulf War was quickly won in the spring of 1991 with few American casualties, especially since Bush decided not to occupy Iraq. In my opinion, this was President Bush's finest moment of his entire political career! He used his seasoned military and political experience to win a swift war against an evil dictator and liberate an important ally in the Middle East. He demonstrated to the world that America will not hesitate to use superior military power for justice. We fight to LIBERATE, not to conquer!

As expected, President Bush and America were delighted and proud that we won a decisive and quick victory in Iraq. Unlike the aftermath of the Vietnam War, our combat soldiers were welcomed home with "yellow ribbons around the old oak trees," marching band parades and concerts. President Bush was quoted as saying, "By God, we've kicked the Vietnam syndrome once and for all." I have very fond memories of our local welcome-home parade in the downtown North Little Rock area that spring of 1991. It was so exciting to see national entertainers such as Bob Hope and Marie Osmond come to town and join the parade with our local brave soldiers. Later that evening, they both performed for a capacity crowd at War Memorial Stadium in Little Rock that included a massive fireworks show, donated by local businessman Jennings Osborne. Bob Hope came to the big stage and delivered an old-school USO-type comedy show that was similar to the Vietnam days that was heart-warming and very entertaining. But what was really historic was when the lovely Marie Osmond called then-Governor Bill Clinton to the stage to sing and dance with her! It was very funny and cool at the same time. Bill was born to be a politician, he loved the big crowd limelight and knew how to entertain folks. He remained a very popular governor for over a decade. Little did I realize that he would announce his presidential campaign against the popular war-winning President Bush later in October, 1991.

Soon after all this national celebration of war victory in the Middle East, President Bush's popularity began to fade for several reasons. He felt forced to break his "no new taxes" pledge when he made compromises with the Democrat-led Congress to raise taxes and make modest budget cuts to avoid larger and across-the-board budget cuts by 1991 that was mandated by the 1985 Graham-Rudman Act. Also, the national economy was slowing down and, due to the Reagan-Bush conservative budget policies, state and local governments felt forced to create new taxes. The breaking of Bush's "NO NEW TAXES" promise inflamed many conservatives and the president's lack of direct action to improve the recent recession created the "perfect storm" for his problematic re-election bid.

In late October, 1991, our own Arkansas Governor Bill Clinton made the formal announcement that he was running against President Bush in the 1992 election. I was shocked! As a local elected official, I received a "VIP" invitation to reserve close seating at the beautiful Old State House in downtown Little Rock. As a conservative Reagan-Bush supporter, I was hesitant to attend; after all, I did not want to appear to be a hypocrite. But, as a good friend told me, this event wasn't about me, it was about

Clinton's historic announcement and I needed to attend and remain respectful. I took his advice and attended the Clinton presidential announcement and indeed the special VIP seating was excellent. We were just a few rows back from the stage. The warm-up speakers came out and delivered the typical background info about the candidate that, of course, we already knew. It was exciting to see all the national press corps and their fancy equipment there, and the crowd of mainly Democrats were getting stirred up. Then, the big moment arrived! The Clinton family came out on the stage and the crowd exploded with excitement! The '70s' rock tune "Yesterday's Gone" by Fleetwood Mac began to blare from the speakers. It became obvious to me that Clinton would use the baby boomer theme of "youth and new beginnings" versus the old age and military/conservative experience of President Bush.

I noticed something really weird about the Clintons - they all looked so different! Bill's hair had suddenly turned "mature-looking" silver-gray overnight, Hillary had a totally new Hollywood makeover, and their young daughter Chelsie looked scared to death! Bill and family had now entered   the big-time game of national politics, their high-end consultants and liberal

Hollywood buddies had taken over, and good-ole-Arkansas would soon be a distant memory. DC, here they come!

As Clinton proceeded with his slick and well-delivered (as usual) stump speech, I was thinking that there is no way he can beat a popular war-winning incumbent President Bush, especially being from a small southern state like Arkansas! I now know that I was dead wrong. With the unexpected help of outspoken billionaire Ross Perot, the great American public servant, businessman, and World War II hero George H. W. Bush would sadly lose his re-election bid to the young Governor Bill Clinton in November 1992. "Baby boomer leadership" in America had officially begun.

Bill Clinton and Al Gore made their mark in two unique ways: they were the first "baby boomer" and all-southern national ticket in American history and, they were also the first non-World War II veterans to run for the White House in over 40 years.

As I now reflect on my March, 1992, trip to the National League of Cities convention in Washington DC, this unfortunate political event makes more sense to me. On the final day of the convention in the large ballroom at the DC Hilton hotel (same location where Reagan was shot in 1981), the keynote speaker was none other than President Bush. Our local delegation had a nice central seating spot about ten rows back, and a city councilman peer of mine that was on the national board was seated at the head table and had the privilege of shaking hands with the president as he concluded his speech (he happened to be a Clinton Democrat, but demonstrated proper respect for the office.) Yes, as a Republican conservative Bush fan, I admit it - I was a tad jealous because I would have loved to have been seated at the head table that day. But, we still had a great view of President Bush and it was very exciting to be in that moment in history. His speech was pretty basic and scripted as he reviewed a broad laundry list of administration achievements and how it helped our urban constituents, but he mainly stressed a stable economy and the new "world order" after winning the Cold War. Frankly, his speech did not receive rave reviews from most of my aldermen and mayor friends that day, even from some of my more conservative friends. Being objective, the president looked tired and a bit burned out. He did not excite or inspire many folks in that fancy ballroom that day. For the first time, I realized that ole smiling Bill from little Arkansas may have a shot at winning, especially as he continued to roll in the Democrat primaries that spring.

The fall, 1992, election was also personal for me. That August, I decided to announce my intention to run for re-election to my city council seat since my original four-year term was winding down. I enjoyed the work and I was proud of my accomplishments in office that included sponsoring over thirty pieces of local legislation in the areas of ethics, crime control, needed public works projects, and aggressive "pro-business" zoning/economic development.

The same night that I was watching Bill Clinton's victory speech back at the Old State House on TV, it was with a heavy heart that I learned that my re-election campaign was in a run-off situation that would extend the campaign for another two weeks. Even though we had a sizeable lead, we narrowly lost the run-off election that was held during the "sacred" deer hunting season period that greatly reduced my voter turnout and I was very disappointed. Later that night I had a sudden flashback from a brief chat I had with Governor Clinton at a Christmas party a few years back while discussing the challenges of young people in politics. Being the youngest Governor in the country at the time,

I thought he could offer me some good advice on this subject. He told me this while he was sipping from his Diet Coke, "Yeah, it's not easy being the youngest guy in your political circle, just keep on working to make your case. It hurts like hell to lose an election." He was referring to his earlier losses to Congressman Hammerschmidt back in the '70s and his upset defeat to former Governor Frank White in 1980. Bill had earned the political nickname of "The Comeback Kid." Bill Clinton was truly born to be a politician.

During those eight years of the Clinton administration, I had a lot of mixed emotions. I certainly disagreed with his more liberal views that coincided with the national Democrat Party, but it was also interesting to learn about a lot of people that worked for him in Washington DC who were from Arkansas. This "small southern state" had never received this sort of national attention, and I remained frustrated that many of my more moderate friends maintained a blind loyalty (almost worship) of Bill and Hillary regardless of their actions. Just because he was "our boy" from good ole Arkansas, I knew this geographical bias was not healthy for our state in the long run.

After Hillary failed with the national healthcare reform effort and over-stepping the traditional role of the First Lady, the "Clinton magic" was starting to fade. Also, the controversial passage of NAFTA angered many union supporters, the Whitewater real estate scandal back home was ugly and the nickname "Slick Willie" was re-emerging. The 1994 mid-term election was a disaster for the Democrats when the Republicans regained control of Congress, and conservative new Speaker of the House Newt Gingrich led the right-wing charge with the "Contract with America" doctrine. I remember celebrating when I learned all the details. This new conservative agenda forced the Clinton administration to start meaningful compromises to reduce the bloated social welfare programs, improve anti-crime programs, cut taxes for the middle-class, reduce expensive federal regulations, and to seriously work on a balanced federal budget. These new developments were great for the country, but also turned out to be a hidden political blessing for President Clinton. I remember so well watching the State of the Union address on TV during the winter of 1996 when the president proclaimed "The era of big government is over!" He then continued to ask the conservative Congress to help him and the country to reduce the national welfare system and finally balance the budget. It was almost shocking to hear these words from a historically liberal Democrat!

These savvy political moves from Clinton swept him back in the White House for another four years when he easily defeated Senator Bob Dole in 1996. Dole was another great example of a fine public servant and wounded World War II hero from the "greatest generation," but he lacked the charisma and youthful energy of the Clinton team. The baby boomer "torch of leadership" was already passed on, and most Americans didn't look back. The national economy was rocking along fine again. This was about the same time that the internet and the "dot.com" economic boom hit in America. I remember how fascinated we were back then when personal computers became common at home and at the workplace…this email thing was even faster than fax machines! My parents were especially mind-blown when I told them that you could now send email messages anywhere in the world instantly….and with the "world wide web" you could research virtually anything in just a few moments! My "old school" Dad responded, "Why, that's impossible! Sorry, son, I just don't believe it!"

Even with this lucky timing of technological events, Clinton ran into new trouble in 1998 when the Monica Lewinsky sex scandal broke. This sad event was embarrassing for the country, especially for my home folks in Arkansas. I knew when this news broke that we would be in for a bitter impeachment fight in Washington DC. My conservative friends were beyond outraged, and even some of my more moderate Democrat friends told me, "I'm done with Bill and 'Hill'. I never really cared about their personal lives in the past, but this latest news goes beyond morality - it's just plain stupid."

At this same time period, I was working in a state government office as a compliance investigator. About half of the office were former Governor Clinton employees, and about half started there under the more recent Governor Mike Huckabee. This "Monica mess" was the main daily office gossip during lunch and break periods, even though we were instructed "not to talk about politics at work" from our supervisors, which I found humorous because most folks that work in state government offices are very political.

As I expected, Clinton was impeached in the Republican-led House, but was acquitted in the Senate due to a lack of widespread public support. Our powerful former Arkansas Democrat governor and US Senator Dale Bumpers presented an emotional speech of support for his ole pal President Clinton, arguing that these sins were a "personal mistake," but did not meet the criteria of "high crimes and misdemeanors" as mandated by the US Constitution.

Throughout the late 1990s, I decided not to run again for any new elective offices, but I stayed involved in local political campaigns and volunteered for civic board and commission work. My good friend Mayor Hays appointed me to a three-year term on the Pulaski County Metroplan 20/20 board which was interesting and educational. We made detailed recommendations for future large expensive transportation and infrastructure projects that would later be funded by using a federal/state tax-matching formula. It has been rewarding to see a lot of those recommendations become a reality.

During my late thirties and early forties, I decided to return to white-collar office work during the week, and continued to practice my blue-collar skills earning money on the weekend. By the end of this decade life was changing dramatically in America with the expansion of the internet and social media platforms.

Wireless "cellular phones" became the latest miracle in technology, and soon they became a basic commodity similar to landline phones back in the day. As I am approaching "middle age" during this time period, my faith in the American free-enterprise system is reinforced. Even with the political scandals and social problems, America continued to move forward, our wonderful country continued to survive and was about to enter a brand new century.

I cannot ever remember a PERFECT America,

but I do remember a BETTER America!

CHAPTER 6

A New Century Begins

In late 1999, "Clinton fatigue" was settling in across the country after the unpleasant impeachment mess, and the next non-incumbent presidential election of year 2000 was fast approaching. Soon came the next big challenge for America to overcome, the very scary reality of Y2K!

At the same time citizens were enjoying all the widespread benefits of the internet, wireless phones, satellite/cable TV, and computerization in general, high tech experts warned the public about a very serious potential programming disaster. For decades now, computer programmers used a two-digit field to describe dates, for example the year 1960 would just be "60." But what would happen in year 2000 when the field suddenly changed to three digits? Y2K was shorthand for Year 2000, and experts feared that this sudden programming change on a mass global scale could possibly cause a catastrophic crash, resulting in losing a vast amount of critical data. The mass media took this "gloom and doom" scenario very seriously. They reminded us 24/7 on cable TV news that Y2K could be the end of our modern society as we knew it. After all, computerization was no longer considered a fancy luxury, but was a vital necessity for banking, utilities, traffic/air control, daily business/educational functions, and even our national defense! I also remember some folks were trying to scam their way to Y2K prosperity through fear, over-selling items such as wood stoves for heat, expensive emergency food supplies for their storm/bomb shelters, hand-cranked radios that did not require electricity, and automatic weapons to use for the "pending rioting and chaos." As a pro-business conservative, I don't mind people making a profit for any of these items normally, but it did irritate me at the time to see business people grossly exaggerate and exploit this situation through fear tactics. Thankfully, thousands of educated and hard-working programmers around the world worked together to solve the problem and we avoided a global disaster. We were all celebrating that New Year's Day!

After the relief of the Y2K crisis, conservatives were looking forward to the end of the Clinton era in year 2000, even though VP Al Gore was quickly becoming the new Democrat nominee.

In the winter/spring period of year 2000, I enjoyed watching the scrappy Republican primary race between powerful senator and Vietnam War hero John McCain and Texas Governor George W. Bush, son of former President H. W. Bush. I initially thought McCain would win this nomination, but the younger and more energetic Governor Bush was a better communicator and ran a better campaign.

The year 2000 turned out to be a life-altering time period for me. Shortly after I was transitioning from a state government compliance job to a county government public relations position, my wife and life partner of over 20 years, mother of my only child, suddenly told me she wanted a divorce. I was shocked and devastated. Our son was finishing the 11th grade at a private school and was about to be awarded a full academic college scholarship. I was very much against getting a divorce, but her decision was already made and it became legally final by the end of that summer. I never before understood when men complained about going through a "mid-life crisis," but now it made sense to me. This quickly became MY mid-life crisis. At age 43, I basically had to start my life all over again….find a new place to live, split up all the household resources down to the family photos and kitchen crockpots, but the worst part was not being able to live with my son anymore.

The next few months were lonely and depressing and, frankly, I became disillusioned about life in general. My Christian "greatest generation" parents were supportive about the situation, but divorce was a foreign word to them; they simply did not believe in divorce unless there was some abuse involved. My dad was especially sympathetic and saddened, but I remember he told me, "Son, divorce is a horrible thing, but you must press on with life." Press on I did, going to work every day and pondering what the future might bring, and reminding myself that I still live in the best country in the world, and that new opportunities would come my way.

The Christmas season of 2000 was a huge personal adjustment for me. For the first time in over twenty years, I was a bachelor again living in a different house than the one I purchased with my now ex-wife back in 1989. I was really missing all the family holiday traditions that we enjoyed during my younger years, and even though I started to casually date again, I felt alone and lost most of the time. When I went to bed at night I wondered why divorce was now so common in America, and how had other people (both men and women) dealt with these same emotions of loneliness and despair? My son was now a senior in high school and about to turn eighteen, and he was excited to secure that full academic college scholarship. I knew it was important to maintain a close relationship with him because he was, without a doubt, the most important person in the world to me. Even though we maintained regular visitation within the same urban area, it still hurt that we were now living in different homes, our traditional nuclear family structure was now broken. I had to accept that he was a grown young adult and was about to make his own way in the world. Indeed, he did just that…. he became a successful Doctor of Physical Therapy and now has a beautiful family of his own.

The historic and controversial presidential election in November 2000 between George W. Bush and VP Al Gore was one for the ages - you could not write a movie script to match this craziness! It was the closest presidential election in American history, even closer than the 1960 Kennedy-Nixon race. Finally, late in the night, the network folks called the win for Bush. I was excited to see another Bush Republican returning to the White House. But wait! A few minutes later they reported a problem with the Florida voting system that put Bush over the top and, ironically, Bush's brother Jeb just happened to be the current governor of Florida. Later, Gore claimed victory which added to the   public confusion. Even later in the night, the TV folks announced that the Florida voting controversy had turned into an absurd state of affairs - a statewide recount was mandated, and we were told we would not know the winner of the presidential race until probably several days later, that it was just too close to call. What was really hard to believe was that this manual hand count of Florida "voting chads" took about another month. Critics called it a circus atmosphere, and finally the US Supreme Court ordered the recount to end and the Florida electoral votes were awarded to Bush, making him the next president.

Conservative Republicans celebrated, liberal Democrats were outraged. However, I was impressed when watching VP Gore's concession speech afterward when he stated that, while he disagreed with the whole Florida decision process, he respected the rule of law within our democracy and he accepted the outcome; it was time for the country to move forward.

Shortly after that very unusual and historic presidential election, another unexpected challenge came our way in the Little Rock metro area. On Christmas night, 2000, a severe ice/sleet storm hit our area that virtually crippled homes and offices. We suffered widespread and long-term power outages, and the local governments and utility companies were completely overwhelmed. The temperatures also remained unusually cold for this area and did not allow for any ice thawing. About a week later, another, separate, ice storm hit that made conditions even worse. I remember that local conditions and communication blackouts were so severe that the mayor and city council members rode around neighborhoods in their own trucks in the freezing cold trying to help people with their basic needs. The general public were uncomfortable and unhappy, but after about two weeks conditions began to improve. After everything returned to normal, Mayor Hays created a new task force/emergency committee in the winter of 2001 to analyze this local disaster and make new recommendations for improvement. I accepted this new volunteer appointment and also met my future wife there. Becky happened to also be a volunteer committee member, and our previous friendship turned romantic. We married the next summer of 2002. It's hard to believe now, but that was over twenty years ago. I guess everything in life really does happen for a reason. My middle-aged life was now renewed!

While the country was swinging back to the right-wing governance of another Bush in the White House, I was still adjusting to the middle-age life of a county government employee. I enjoyed my new role in public relations and I often gave luncheon speeches to civic groups and other local organizations regarding the role of our office and services offered. We also started giving brief presentations to local schools educating young students about the role of government and how it interacts with business to keep our society running smoothly. Most of my peers and friends in local government were not crazy about having another Bush in the White House, there were many Clinton-Gore Democrats working in the system who believed that the new president was too simple-minded and focused on big business rather than helping our local taxpayers. I avoided conflicts and just did my job. The Democrats and the media also started to criticize the new "Bush II" administration for governing to the far-right which contradicted his campaign promise of being a "moderate." They were especially critical of the president's inner circle of VP Dick Cheney, advisor Karl Rove, and Republican Congressional Whip Tom DeLay who declared "all-out war" on the Democrats.

One morning at my office I was routinely watching the news. My boss had authorized a small television in my office to keep on cable news network to stay informed with current events. As I watched TV on that dark day, September 11, 2001, I saw the historic terrorist attacks on our country! I watched in shock and horror as the planes crashed into the World Trade Center in New York City, then the Pentagon in DC. There was news of a third plane crash in Pennsylvania. It was surreal to me. How could this happen to the mighty United States of America? And how could anybody in this world be so ruthless and cruel?

Later that morning, around lunch time, the county government CEO ordered all employees to go upstairs to the main meeting room for an emergency meeting. He was, of course, furious and horrified at these tragic events, as we all were. He informed us that our country was indeed under terrorist attack, and the governor of Arkansas had just informed him of preplanned emergency procedures within the entire state government system that coincided with a national emergency.

They did not know yet the full extent of the attack and we were told that some of these response plans were "classified." That word "classified" got my attention. He also stated that we were "all government public servants" and subject to being "federalized" during a national emergency. That literally sent chill bumps of caution and fear up my spine.

Becky and I were dating, and she phoned my office concerned for our safety since we were in a government building. At that moment, I told her not to worry - but after I learned more details of the terrorists' evil and sadistic motives against our American government, I shared her concerns. I never dreamed on that horrible day that six years later I would be teaching detailed high school lessons on 9-11 and the now-famous "war on terror" that evolved into the "endless wars" of Iraq and Afghanistan. These evil terrorists were very symbolic - they wanted to destroy the World Trade Center to demonstrate they could bring down our financial strength. The Pentagon attack symbolized the defeat of our military might, and the plane that crashed in Pennsylvania was headed either for the Capitol or the White House, symbolizing the defeat of our political power. This was truly a sick plot against humanity!

I remember watching that famous visit President Bush made on September 14 to the World Trade Center "ground zero" area. He embraced rescue workers while standing on the building rubble, took a bullhorn, publicly declared a "war on terror," and promised to carry the battle to terrorist networks known as Al Qaeda. He then spoke to a joint session of Congress and told the nation that America was now at war, and swift military action would be taken against these terrorist networks.

Most outraged Americans supported this military action, and a new wave of patriotism swept the country. I vividly remember the large newspaper headlines that soon followed: "AMERICA STRIKES BACK" above a large picture of cruise missiles being fired from an American aircraft carrier. People of all walks of life started a new wave of posting American flags symbolizing their united support for the new war on terror. There were flag decals on car bumpers, flag decals on college and pro football helmets, posters on glass store fronts, and even large flags waving from pickup trucks. America seemed united once again. By early 2002, the bombing of terrorist camps in Afghanistan greatly reduced resistance, but mastermind Osama bin Laden escaped to nearby Pakistan – as the most hated man in America. Many more moderate national leaders urged Bush to declare post 9-11 victory, to wrap up the new war before it escalated, and to continue to track down bin Laden as a separate Special Forces mission. But the president and his very conservative inner circle advisors rejected that advice, and moved forward with broad domestic actions via the USA Patriot Act, allowing warrantless phone wiretaps, government monitoring of banking transactions, and giving the administration new authority to attack any dangerous states, even absent any imminent threat, all in the name of "national security." This new foreign policy philosophy was called "The Bush Doctrine." Soon afterward, the president ordered the military invasion of Iraq in 2003, named "Operation Iraqi Freedom" to remove the dictator Saddam Hussein from power.

It was around this time that President Bush II started to lose me. Like most Americans, I had no love for the evil dictator Hussein, but as I watched our US Army tanks begin to invade the borders of Iraq based on the speculation of finding "weapons of mass destruction" (WMD's), I became very concerned. This aggressive military action appeared to be over the top because there was not an obvious immediate threat to our national security at the time. On the other hand, did I trust Hussein and/or his dictator thugs? Absolutely not! But I thought the public and the world should at least see more intelligence evidence before starting another protracted war, similar to what President Kennedy made public during the 1962 Cuban Missile Crisis. There was some evidence later presented that Hussein might have been in the beginning stages of developing WMD's, but to me this was a very weak argument to justify a new military invasion of Iraq. In later years, this decision appeared to be very reckless for our nation as it was indeed the beginning of the "endless wars" that haunted us for two decades.

As the Iraqi insurgencies and internal ethnic conflicts became more apparent, entrenching our country into a long-term ground war, I was reminded of President Johnson's mistakes in Vietnam. Critics were beginning to ask if Bush II had an exit strategy to end this war.

During this 2003/04 time period I was also working on my first master's degree in public administration at Webster University (Little Rock Air Force Base location) at night which was very research-intensive. There were several young Air Force officers also attending this program that were super sharp and very patriotic. The current war situation was a controversial hot topic during class discussions and research presentations, but students remained professional and respectful. However, one thing was clear: everyone in those night classes was concerned that our country was headed in the wrong direction regarding the war on terror.

The now-famous "9-11 Commission Report" was brand new back then, and it was required reading. It was very long and complex, but the basic conclusion of this commission was that the 9-11 tragedy occurred because of widespread communication problems within our government and intelligence communities, including negative internal "turf battles."

Heading into the 2004 presidential election, the president appeared to be in trouble due to the mess in Iraq, critics were clamoring that America appeared to now be "invading occupiers" instead of "liberators," and Democrats and the media were beating the administration over the head regarding the lack of evidence of Iraqi "weapons of mass destruction." After a very spirited campaign on both sides, President Bush II managed to defeat liberal Massachusetts Senator John Kerry in November, 2004. What I remember the most about that campaign season was the "Swift Boat Veterans for Truth" TV ads. Just when Kerry was in striking distance for a victory, these ads featured some of his Vietnam War peers charging that Kerry lied about his combat actions to win his medals. The ads showing a long-haired young image of Kerry protesting the war made Kerry appear to be unpatriotic. This negative image, and his well-documented and inconsistent left-wing voting record in the Senate, ensured his defeat. In post-election interviews, voters told interviewers that President Bush II "made them feel safe," despite growing concerns about the war on terror dragging on.

The president now felt vindicated being re-elected to a second term, and pressed on with a very conservative agenda of pro-life and anti-stem cell research policies, appointing two new conservative judges to the Supreme Court: John Roberts in 2005 (who later was considered somewhat liberal) and Samuel Alito in 2006. After the Congressional reauthorization of the Patriot Act in 2006, it was full steam ahead for more war activities and the ongoing erosion of American civil liberties.

As the country was becoming more war weary of the protracted conflicts in the Middle East, unexpected domestic problems continued in America. In the summer of 2005, the historic Category 5 Hurricane Katrina devastated the Gulf Coast region, especially in the New Orleans area. Those now-famous images of the president flying over the area surveying the damage from his airplane window were certainly an unintended public relations blunder. The critical media were very unfair that day, in my opinion, falsely accusing Bush of being uncaring and lazy as "he looked down at the people," insinuating that he was apathetic regarding their critical needs. He later stated that he wanted to stay out of the way of the relief efforts and would announce new recovery plans soon. Indeed, I remember the president holding a live TV press conference in New Orleans soon after and pledged a massive multi-billion dollar relief package. It was later discovered that the mayor of New Orleans was tardy in his official duties requesting federal aid, and it was not the fault of the Bush administration that FEMA relief was slow arriving to the area. President Bush was treated very unfairly during this sequence of events by the media and the Democrats.

This was about the same time period that I started a new career as a professional educator in Little Rock. I remember so well that the school district announced a new program to help Katrina-affected families and their kids to re-locate to the central Arkansas area. The hurricane devastation was so severe that many schools in the area closed or were destroyed. I met new students from the area that told me that the TV pictures did not capture how bad the conditions were, especially in the New Orleans area. One young man told me, "You just have to see it in person to wrap your head around it - it looks like a disaster movie down there." My wife and I also had a new rental tenant from the Gulf area east of New Orleans that fall. Their home had been totally destroyed and they were awarded a FEMA rental relief voucher. They were very quiet and decent tenants, but I remember how depressed and empty they looked. After about nine months they left one day without notice. They left the house clean and mailed back the keys with a short note: "Gone back home."

As President Bush was winding down his last couple of years in office, like so many other presidents, his influence was starting to fade, especially with a now war-weary public. In the 2006 second mid-term congressional election, Democrats regained control of Congress and made life more difficult for conservatives. They continued to heavily criticize the lack of a war exit strategy, and they did not agree with Bush's 2007 "war surge strategy" that added about 20,000 more troops in Iraq. Powerful

Republican Senator John McCain had supported this move, and he later became the Republican presidential nominee in 2008 against Barack Obama.

Another huge program of the Bush II administration that directly affected me as a new public   educator was the federal "No Child Left Behind Act" (NCLBA). At the time, this huge piece of bureaucracy seemed like a sound idea to me, we all want our kids to learn and grow, and we all want our kids and school teachers to be held accountable, right? But I quickly learned as a public school teacher that the federal NCLBA was a total fiasco in practice. Once again, even with the best intentions and goals, if you want something totally screwed up, let the federal government get involved! The main reason this program was a total failure and was eventually revised, was that it placed an unrealistic testing burden on both students and teachers, was very complex and expensive, and it created a false sense of testing accountability even when test scores rose. Moreover, this overzealous legislation created an overly punitive mandate that motivated school districts across the country to "teach to the tests," thereby reducing time to teach needed critical thinking skills. The bottom line to the NCLBA was that it did more harm than good to students, teachers, and parents, and basically gave conservative educational managers a bad name. It also contradicted the long-standing conservative philosophy of "local control" versus large federal mandates.

Due to these very unpopular Republican programs, I felt the country begin to sway back to the left. The magic of the Reagan-Bush years were just about gone, and younger folks and many political moderates were searching for something new and exciting. Soon there came a slick-talking inexperienced young Senator from Chicago with the unusual name of "Barack." His message was simple in 2008. His "Hope and Change" campaign theme evolved into the proposed "fundamental transformation of America," but this was not the hope and change that America needed. It quickly became a Socialist nightmare for our country that will be discussed in the next chapter.

I cannot ever remember a PERFECT America,

but I do remember a BETTER America!

# CHAPTER 7

Obama and Big Government

During the fall of 2008, the daily news was painful to watch. The end of the Bush II administration was coming to a close on a very negative note - a major collapse in our national financial system that started a period known as "The Great Recession." This name alone reminded senior citizens such as my parents of the hard times during the "Great Depression" they remembered as children, and alarmed most folks that this situation was serious and historic. It was caused by a complex series of economic mistakes and unethical behavior within the real estate/mortgage industries, and it sent Wall Street into a temporary meltdown. President Bush II tried to summarize the situation in a speech he gave on national TV, claiming that his administration officials were ahead of the curve to avoid a new economic depression. But many people I knew back then were not impressed when they witnessed sudden mass job layoffs that, indeed, thrusted the country into a deep recession. The bottom line was that liberals blamed the excessive financial de-regulation policies of Republicans for the downturn, and conservatives viewed these policies as short-term market corrections that would help the economy in the long-run. Bush tried to justify these loose mortgage lending practices as a positive method to increase home ownership among the lower income classes. The reality was that millions of newer home loans were too risky and simply failed, causing an economic calamity within the large housing/banking industries that had a widespread negative impact on the general economy. I knew that Republicans were in trouble that fall when the president told the public he was meeting with both presidential candidates in private (Senators Barack Obama and John McCain) to discuss detailed action plans that were needed after he left office in January, 2009. The Democrats and the Obama campaign took advantage of this bad news, and they won the 2008 election by a solid margin.

In the fall of 2008 I was starting a new teaching assignment in a middle school within the same district. After three challenging years teaching in a strict "alternative ed" environment, I was ready for a change. I also taught within the after-school and summer tutoring/enrichment programs to earn extra money and gain more educational experience. This was time well spent for students and teachers. We helped a lot of struggling kids with their routine homework and special projects, and it was also an opportunity to get to know your students better in a more relaxed atmosphere, usually in small groups. In addition, we taught these inner-city kids how to play chess and other educational games that were fun and helped to develop their critical thinking skills in a quiet environment. What I remember most about that fall of 2008 was how jubilant my kids were when Obama won the election. I tried to teach them about the larger issues in an objective manner (social studies/history class) of that campaign but, frankly, most of them just wanted Obama to win because he was African- American. I understood that to a certain extent, but I was disappointed that his race was their only focus. I wanted them to learn the importance of studying the political issues, regardless of the candidates' race, gender, or religion.

The day after the election, I had routine cafeteria supervision duty during the lunch hour and I noticed the kids were especially happy and excited, which I expected. Then I noticed something else unusual when the kids were going through the lunch lines. Most of them had a new purple temporary face tattoo that read in capital letters, "YES WE CAN", copying an Obama campaign slogan. After I pondered on that message, I suddenly had a deeper understanding of Obama's emotional appeal to African-Americans, especially to young people. Even though they did not study the detailed issues that I had hoped for, they certainly understood the overall historical significance of the first elected African-American US president.

As painful as the campaign was for me to watch, Obama's performance as president was even more disappointing. It quickly became obvious to me that America was taking a sharp turn to the left, and a new era of big government socialism was beginning. Early in February, 2009, President Obama signed the "American Recovery & Reinvestment Act" to stimulate the recessionary economy. Leaders on both sides of the aisle agreed that the new recession was so deep that some government stimulus was warranted, but this legislation was too expensive and wasteful. The intent was to create infrastructure-related jobs quickly, but we soon learned that few "shovel-ready" projects were actually included in this massive bill, and that it was bloated with "green new deal" type projects that coincided with Obama's left-wing failed environmental policies. I remember witnessing wasteful spending myself during this time period: a lot of extra school supplies not being used, fencing projects that appeared to be cosmetic rather than for security, a road project near my rural home that appeared to be unnecessary but to simply straighten out a slight curve….and who could forget those famous "Obama wireless phones" that the feds were giving away on street corners!

As the Great Recession dragged on, this wasteful spending bill did not appear to be helping the general economy much as more waste and fraud were being discovered. Then, the new healthcare debate rekindled from the Clinton days and Obama started to lobby Congress for a big government universal health insurance bill that conservatives were very much against. He proposed that every American should be mandated to have health insurance coverage through the federal government, regardless of their pre-existing conditions. He insisted that enacting this new massive federal program would improve the overall health condition of our citizens, and lower the overall coats of healthcare, especially in the long run. Conservatives strongly disagreed for a variety of sound reasons. It would give the federal government excessive power over the personal health decisions of millions of Americans; it would destroy many high quality private health insurance programs that people were satisfied with, including many union labor plans, and it would reduce the overall quality of health care, thereby raising costs to most people.

In March, 2010, the "Patient Protection and Affordable Care Act" was passed in Congress and signed into law by the president. This huge piece of complex and expensive legislation was referred to as "Obamacare." It passed Congress without a single Republican vote, and I remember so well watching House Speaker Nancy Pelosi march arrogantly to the Capitol Hill steps with a huge ceremonial gavel, along with her fellow Democrats and their smug smiles of confidence, which proved to me that the vote was already a "done deal." They did not care that most Americans and EVERY Republican member of Congress opposed this massive disruption to our healthcare system, they were only concerned with their selfish power-crazed left-wing socialist agenda! This ill-advised legislation also gave excessive new enforcement power to the IRS to issue new fines for any taxpayer that did not enroll in federal Obamacare - a disgraceful example of government over-reach that was later repealed by the Trump administration. Yes, some lower-income Americans were now with new health insurance, but many more citizens suffered sudden cost increases, or even lost their existing private insurance as well as losing their choice of specific doctors and/or hospitals - a blatant broken promise made by President Obama during the debates. Ironically, I was diagnosed with the early stages of prostate cancer during this time period but, thankfully, I was able to be fully cured via a series of radiation treatments at a nearby hospital over a period of about ten weeks. I was thankful that my quality employer-provided health insurance covered most of the expensive treatment costs.

Shortly after the shock of Obamacare becoming the new law of the land, a tragic accident rocked the nation: the historic British Petroleum (BP) oil spill disaster that caused major damage to the Southern Gulf region, and killed 11 workers and injured another 17 workers due to an oil well "blowout" explosion in April, 2010. Private and public sectors immediately began rescue and cleanup operations. This accident caused billions of dollars in environmental and property damage. On June 15, 2010, President Obama went on national TV to address the tragedy and inform the public of new actions that were being taken by his administration. At the time, I agreed that it was appropriate to take action to help with the cleanup and rescue operation, but what I noticed later was that the president was using this human tragedy to promote an anti-oil company position, and to start pitching his "climate change" agenda. After reviewing the actual text of his speech, one of his statements concerned me: "We need to build an organization that acts as the oil industry's watchdog, not its partner." Most people realize and agree that the big oil industries are heavily regulated and spend vast amounts of money related to safety and environmental regulations, and that they are the last people who would ever want to cause such a tragic human accident.

My older brother grew up to be a highly educated and successful petroleum engineer/executive. I could not resist asking his professional opinion regarding the BP disaster. He stated the following to me via email: "The oil companies go to great expense and training to insure safety, both personal and environmental, but there are times that accidents in all shapes and forms occur.

The oil companies provide the energy needs of the US and the world and they spend   great sums of money and take on great financial risk to accomplish this task. In the case of the BP spill, BP and supporting players spent large, and I mean large, sums of money to abate the environmental, physical and psychological impacts of the accident. Ultimately, I think all environmental impacts have been mitigated and BP stepped up to the plate to address the issues involved. The big oil companies don't take anything like this lightly. They hate the negative impacts worse than anyone."

Shortly after the BP disaster, as the nation was catching their breath, President Obama approved another massive and complex piece of legislation known as the Dodd-Frank Wall Street Reform and Consumer Protection Act in July 2010. This bill was over 23,000 pages long, and it was clearly the largest banking/financial reform package since the Great Depression. The country was still in a deep recession due to the financial crash of 2008, and leaders from both sides of the aisle agreed that concrete actions should be taken to avoid another financial disaster. The new regulations were so involved and complex to implement, leaders knew it would take time to notice any positive changes to the economy.

We now know there were several positive and negative long-term results.

Generally speaking, the most positive improvements were in the form of daily consumer protections from overly aggressive "predator" type mortgage and credit card loans. These were unethical because lenders knew that many of these loans would default and cause harm to the economy, and these bad practices were a major cause of the financial crisis. This bill also included a wide variety of changes made to bank credit ratings, "derivatives"/default swaps, it ended abuses of high-interest payday loans used by many lower-income citizens, and strengthened whistleblower provisions in reporting illegal and/or unethical behavior within the financial community. The president and Democrats were excited to deliver these positive reforms that sounded really good when first announced, but like so many other liberal Democrat policies, these new regulations went too far and indeed had several negative and unintended consequences. These new broad regulations were complex and expensive to implement. They required banks to hold more cash assets that reduced business investment opportunities, they decreased overall corporate profits that reduced global competitiveness and, by maintaining less cash reserves, it limited the bond market. Moreover, in May, 2018, Congress passed the "Economic, Regulatory Relief, and Consumer Protection Act" which removed the Volcker Rule to make smaller community banks more competitive. This highlighted the over-regulation of Dodd-Frank.

The other main failures of this Democrat-led financial effort were that the number of subprime loans written by federally managed lenders Freddie Mac and Fannie Mae were not significantly reduced, and the pace of the general economic recovery remained slow. Once again, even when our leaders have the best goals and intentions, when they enact overly broad government regulations suddenly upon the private sector it usually results in decreased production and profits that damage our economy and quality of life.

During this same time period I have to admit that I was somewhat distracted from the news because I made the decision to start working on my second master's degree in educational leadership at my beloved undergraduate school, the University of Central Arkansas in Conway. This program was also very research-intensive, but it was designed for working teachers to attend night classes to obtain their school principal/ administrator's license. The professors were wonderful. Not only did most of them hold their PHD credentials, they also had years of professional teaching and administrating experience. They knew how to implement deep academic principles into modern schools and classrooms. I was also impressed with their professional demeanor. Some were conservative and some were "classical liberal" as we discussed the current politics of the educational business. Most of my class peers expressed somewhat liberal viewpoints when engaging in class discussions and research presentations, but they remained courteous and respectful when I expressed more conservative views that criticized the misguided policies of Obama, and the current public-school systems in general.

This was about the same time when the radical "critical race theory" controversy first started in teacher professional development (PD) seminars. I knew very nice teachers who thought this made sense because they believed that we needed to confront our inherent racial prejudices and admit that America was "founded on slavery." My response was always, "Who have you been listening to? America was NOT founded on slavery! It was founded on our precious freedoms and democratic republic principles, documented by our sacred US Constitution and Bill of Rights! In all my years, I have   never known a single person from any background who did not agree that the institution of slavery in America was a total travesty of justice. We all know that it was simply wrong. But the US Constitution allowed our post-Civil War leaders to correct that injustice…. it's called the 13th Amendment." I proudly completed my second master's degree in 2012, with honors, and I was later promoted to   an assistant principal position at a nearby high school.

Due to the displeasure of many of Obama's big government policies of over spending and excessive regulations (and some Republican mistakes as well) the new American Tea Party was forming   in the fall of 2010 that advocated a much leaner and less-expensive government. Many of these folks were ordinary middle-class workers who were new to the political game, but they knew that Washington DC, in general, was out of control, and they demanded immediate changes, especially with   tax policies.

Republicans took advantage of this new movement, and won the Congressional majority back in the 2010 mid-term election, and suddenly it appeared that President Obama was losing his shine of popularity. Indeed, the new conservative majority began to push back on Obamacare, his new promotion of "global warming" (later called "climate change") environmental programs, and other liberal social policies such as gay marriage and transgender civil rights.

In another huge development, President Obama announced May 1, 2011, on TV, that the evil terrorist Osama bin Laden was killed by US Navy Seals in Pakistan. Of course that was a popular development with most Americans, but later I was personally not impressed when the administration released a bogus-looking "photo op" of the president and his inner circle watching the military mission on a TV screen in the situation room. It looked totally fake to me, and tailor-made for a future campaign commercial. What was even more irritating to me was the failed mission in Benghazi, Libya, on September 11, 2012, at our American embassy. Ambassador Christopher Stephens and three other Americans were killed by terrorists, and Obama officials blatantly lied and blamed the attack on a video that offended local Muslims. Defense Secretary Leon Panetta later admitted that officials knew it was a terrorist attack shortly after it happened, and it had nothing to do with that video, but officials such as Susan Rice and Hillary Clinton continued their false media cover story to avoid responsibility.

Then came the presidential election of 2012. I really thought that President Obama was in   trouble this time - his theme of "hope and change" appeared to be altered to "hope and shame" the way he was running the country. The economy was still weak, even after spending huge amounts of new money via the stimulus bill, the new Dodd-Frank regulations angered most of the banking and business community, most folks hated Obamacare (less coverage with higher costs), and the war in Afghanistan was still raging! On October 3, 2012, President Obama and Republican nominee Mitt Romney engaged in their first TV debate, discussing domestic policies. Romney scored political points when he reminded the president (and a national TV audience) that the country was headed in the wrong direction: "Over 40 million Americans are now on food stamps, Obamacare has been a failure, our economy remains stagnant, our taxes remain too high, and the war in Afghanistan continues to drag on with no end in sight." The president also appeared to be tired and even bored, his debate responses were not the least bit convincing, and afterward even my Democrat friends who thought Obama "hung the moon" expressed their disappointment. My wife and I were celebrating in my living room that night because we sincerely thought that Romney had an excellent chance to win that race. We were wrong. Romney and his VP running mate, young Congressman Paul Ryan from Wisconsin, appeared to run out of gas in the home stretch, and President Obama was re-elected by the same basic support base from 2008, even with a weak economy.

In his second term, Barack Obama continued to be a very polarizing figure with his ongoing obsession with race, gender, and religion. He continued to boast about his now-famous Obamacare, even though most Americans did not approve of the long-term results, with less coverage at higher costs. He never apologized for any of his mistakes or blunders. This broken promise: "If you like your health care plan, you can keep your health care plan," was deemed the "2013 Lie of the Year." He once called the ISIS terrorist network the "JV team," and always refused to state the words "Islamic extremists" because he was afraid to offend "ordinary Muslims". His track record regarding government secrecy, spying, and his war on whistleblowers and press reporters was inappropriate. He never took any responsibility whatsoever about the tragedy in Benghazi. His famous quote in 2014 that claimed his administration had "not a smidgen of corruption" is simply inaccurate, especially after the IRS-targeting scandals and the justice department's "fast and furious" gun-smuggling scandal.

Even with these political and social disagreements, life moved on with more important events. In the summer of 2013, my sweet Dad passed away suddenly after a brief illness, and my brother and I had to move my mother to an assisted living facility due to her declining health. The very night before Dad died, I visited him at his hospital room. He was discouraged about his recent surgery and told me he felt that his time for leaving this earth was near. He gazed over at the whiteboard on the wall in the room that evening and noticed the current date, and he told me it was the exact date that he enlisted in the Army in 1952 during the Korean War. He said, "Son, that day seems like yesterday, but I know it was another lifetime ago. Don't ever take a day for granted. Life is short."

Shortly after my father passed away, I retired from the education field and started helping my wife with her promotional products and rental businesses, which I have very much enjoyed. Life soon became even more interesting when we learned that "The Donald" was coming to Little Rock to speak in February, 2016. Those details will be discussed in Chapter 8.

I cannot ever remember a PERFECT America,

but I do remember a BETTER America!

CHAPTER 8

Common Sense Populism with Trump

As the far-left Obama administration was winding down, millions of conservatives and moderate independent voters were starving for new leadership in America. Even though the economy had improved from the depths of the Great Recession of 2008/09, overall recovery was still moving at a snail's pace. After almost seven years of Obama's extreme socialistic policies regarding the Obamacare failures, "climate change" nonsense, and his absurd daily "political correctness" habits, even many of my Democrat friends were ready for a change. I remember so well that we were excited to learn that our popular former Governor Mike Huckabee decided to run for president again in the 2016 election, and the early qualified Republican field of candidates was growing in the summer of 2015. Later that summer came the real game changer for the Republican primaries - none other than American business icon and TV celebrity, Donald J. Trump, announced that he, too, would be a serious Republican candidate for president of the United States! When my wife and I tuned in to watch his announcement speech at the famous Trump Tower in Manhattan, New York, I was super- impressed and immediately thought he would at least win the Republican primary. Trump was already TV and media savvy, and was also very wealthy and famous.… necessary key elements for success in today's modern campaign climate. He also had a simple and bold message that many Americans found refreshing: he promised to improve the economy through tax cuts, de-regulation, and new international trade deals, solve our southern border immigration crisis, and finally win the war on   terror by strengthening our military. He later stressed the importance of "draining the swamp" in Washington DC of corrupt career politicians who were not serving the real needs of most hard-working American taxpayers, he proposed to build the now-famous southern border wall to keep out illegal aliens, and he proposed to end all the political correctness and climate change nonsense from the current Obama administration.

Then the real fun began for politicos: a series of national televised debates of over a dozen Republican candidates in various different locations around the country. Each location changed the debate moderators who offered a variety of political perspectives. I considered most of these candidates to be highly qualified to be the next president, but my three favorites were Governor Huckabee, Texas Senator Ted Cruz and, of course, Donald J. Trump. In full disclosure I have always liked and admired Trump and his family, and found his "non-politician" and "self-funding" campaign status super-refreshing! His brash personality, wealth, bluntness, and inflated ego certainly do NOT offend me in the slightest. But, corrupt career politicians that spend the taxpayer's money with reckless abandon DO offend me, especially the ones that have never had a real private-sector job in their lives!

We enjoyed watching those TV debates throughout the fall of 2015 leading up to the January 2016 primaries. Each one was somewhat different and very informative, but one thing became very clear to me as the candidate field was narrowing down: Trump stole the debate stage and he was the clear front-runner.

He was not the "slickest" speaker, but he was the most engaging speaker. His rhetoric became more and more blunt and honest as the debates began to wind down, his poll numbers continued to climb upward as his message of "common sense populism" was lighting a positive fire under millions of voters. Another memory of those TV debates that stands out in my mind as I reflect is when Trump looked straight into the camera and told the audience, "Look, I'm the only guy up here that really knows how to get this economy going again. I'm the only guy that knows how to stop illegal aliens from destroying our country. I'm the only guy up here that can beat Crooked Hillary Clinton!" The other remaining candidates looked a bit stunned from Trump's bluntness. That's when I was convinced that he would at least be the Republican nominee - he had that winning look of confidence and determination of a future president.

After the actual primary season started in January, we were excited to learn that "The Donald" was planning a campaign rally in Little Rock that February, 2016 – you just needed to register online in advance for seating and security purposes. Then the big day came. My wife and I attended the rally at the old Barton Coliseum. Many secret service and local police officers were there wearing bullet-proof vests, and everything on your person was scanned - similar to entering an airport. We saw a few local conservative celebrities that were proudly carrying large Trump signs, and then I was surprised to see a local Democrat politico friend seated in the stands wearing a ball cap low over his eyes, as if he was hiding. I waved at him and he just slumped down in his seat and smiled. I think he was there just to check out the competition, which I found amusing. After the typical warm-up speakers finished on the main stage, they announced that Trump was just landing in Little Rock and would be there in a few minutes. And, then, there he was. "The Donald" entered the stage area and the crowd went nuts, with the classic Lee Greenwood song "I'm Proud to Be an American" blaring from the loud speakers. It was a surreal moment for us, indeed! Trump began his stump speech and asked for votes before the pending Arkansas' "SEC Super Tuesday" primary. His voice seem louder and bolder in person that it sounded on TV - he was truly larger-than-life that day. During his closing, the crowd went crazy when he simply and bluntly announced in a raised strong voice: "I'm going to bomb the shit out of ISIS!" I turned my head toward my wife and said, "This guy does not mince words, does he?"

After his stump speech was concluded he started an informal question and answer session with the audience, which was even more engaging. I left my seat and went closer to the stage to get a closer look at Trump. I was surprised to notice how much taller and larger he looked than on TV. He answered every single question in detail from the close-up audience and I became more impressed with his command of the issues. Though plain-spoken, Donald Trump is obviously a very intelligent man.

As he was leaving, he made some time to go below the stage to autograph campaign signs and MAGA caps. I noticed Paula Jones (from the famous Bill Clinton sexual harassment case) at the end of the stage shouting "Mr. Trump, Mr. Trump, would you please autograph my sign?" Trump recognized her and shouted back, "I see ya, honey! Hold on, I'm coming down to see you! I got ya, honey." He then autographed her sign and shook her hand. She was thrilled, obviously excited to be supporting Trump in a campaign against Hillary Clinton, who she had won a financial settlement from in the harassment case. Then Trump headed my way down the security line. I was just a few feet away and hoping to get a hand shake – something told me even then that this man was going to be our next president. He signed a young man's MAGA hat right in front of me and I thought this would be my golden opportunity to shake "The Donald's" hand! I reached out my stubby middle-aged hand with enthusiasm……and, drum roll, please…….a big, burly secret service agent pushed me back as Trump made his way toward the exit. CURSES! Oh, well, it was still a wonderful and historic moment in time for me that I will never forget!

After Trump won the majority of Republican delegates in that March, 2016, Super Tuesday primary, it became a two-man race between Trump and Senator Cruz. I remember well watching that night when Trump managed to beat Cruz in the Indiana primary, making Trump the "presumptive nominee" and contradicting the predictions of the so-called experts and political pundits. Who could forget the gross arrogance of the mainstream media types, and even Obama himself, when conservative author Ann Coulter predicted early on that Trump would win the Republican nomination? True to their out-of-touch character, these folks all predicted that there was no way that someone like Trump could ever succeed in politics…he was too blunt, too egotistical, and too inexperienced to ever win a nomination, much less beat a seasoned politician like Hillary Clinton. What was so ironic about this miscalculation was that this same display of DC and Hollywood arrogance was the very reason Trump became our president: the public was craving a non-politician who knew how the real business world operates to solve our problems and to, hopefully, "drain the corrupt DC swamp" in the process.

My family and I were so proud and happy on that November, 2016, election night around 2 a.m. when Donald Trump was finally declared the winner. Trump was the polar opposite of Barack Obama, and that was a great thing for America. The country was truly at a historical crossroads for survival. On that night I reflected on the negative debate performances by Hilary Clinton during the fall, 2016, general election. She appeared arrogant and angry, and by then it was obvious that she rigged the Democrat Primary victory over Bernie Sanders by manipulating "super delegates." But what I really reflected upon was her totally bogus claim that Trump was "Putin's puppet," suggesting that Russian dictator Putin was controlling the Trump campaign, when the reality was just the opposite! There is now substantial evidence that suggests 1) that it was the Clinton campaign that created the false stories of Russian involvement with Trump's organization, 2) that Trump's campaign was spied upon during and after the election period, and 3) that the almost two years of Democrat-led congressional hearings/investigations were a complete waste of taxpayer time and money, and were truly a sham operation that ignored the real problems faced by the American people.

On January 20, 2017, Donald J. Trump became the 45th president of the United States. He began his administration with practical actions that coincided with his campaign promises. On January 27, 2017, he signed an executive order banning travel from seven Muslim-majority nations in an effort to reduce the illegal immigration of suspected terrorists and ignored the false left-wing accusations of   racism. On January 30, 2017, the new president notified member countries of the US withdrawal from the failing Trans-Pacific Partnership (TPP) free trade deal, which started his aggressive new program of   negotiating new trade deals to improve the economy.

In another early bold move, the president announced the US exit from the expensive and unfair Paris Climate Pact, which made sense for America. Later that first summer of the Trump era, foreign leaders, like the eccentric Communist dictator of

North Korea, Kim Jong Un, began testing our new president's resolve. They discovered that Trump means what he says, and says exactly what he means.

Since dictators had become accustomed to the weak-kneed apologetic "blame America first" foreign policy of Obama, they were skeptical about Trump's bold rhetoric. North Korea continued with their provocative and irresponsible testing of missiles that were capable of delivering nuclear weapons to our nearby allies of South Korea and Japan, and they were boasting that they could even target large cities on our west coast. On August 8, 2017, President Trump publically warned North Korea that they will face "fire and fury" if the missile threats continue. And, of course, the liberal media and the Democrats started freaking out that Trump should just keep his "big mouth shut before he starts a nuclear war." And guess what? These threatening actions from North Korea suddenly stopped and, by the next June, Trump and Un met in person for a historic summit in Singapore, which was the first ever summit between the two countries since the Korean War. Even though President Trump was not able to obtain his main goal of a formal missile band treaty, the routine missile testing nonsense stopped, and the threat of war greatly diminished in that region.

During this crucial time in our history, what were the Democrats in Congress most concerned about? RUSSIA, RUSSIA, RUSSIA!!!!! That's right, instead of working with our wonderful and hard-working new president to improving the economy, securing our borders, wrapping up the war on terror, and standing firm against the real enemies of our free democracy, they were obsessed with spreading the totally false narrative of a Trump-Russian collusion plot. Once again, their partners in crime, the biased left-wing media continued to broadcast these absurdities 24/7 in their attempt to poison the minds of voters. We now know after over two years of very expensive and time-consuming congressional investigations, that these allegations were totally false. Recently there is documented evidence that these false rumors originated from the Hillary Clinton campaign back in 2016. This fiasco was a sad chapter in our political history, and the Democrat Party still owes our country a huge apology for this disgraceful waste of time and tax money!

In another brave foreign policy move in May, 2018, President Trump announced the US withdrawal from the very ill-advised

Iran nuclear deal negotiated by former Secretary of State John Kerry. Not only did Trump and the conservative news media expose the outrageous millions of dollars of cash payments to these evil international terrorists' thugs, but Trump also further proved to the world that the Obama administration negotiated from a position of weakness, not strength. Again, his position did not require a master's degree in political science to comprehend his foreign policy doctrine…. he simply stated that Iran's development of a nuclear weapon is totally UNACCEPTABLE, under any circumstances, period. When I watched a video of the Obama administration delivering pallets of cold cash from our government in the secrecy of night, I thought to myself, "How in the world could something so wrong be approved by any American president?" I received the answer when watching Trump back on the campaign stump heading into the 2018 mid-term election: "I have learned since being president that in recent years our international deals have been negotiated by stupid people."

Later in the summer of 2018, a so-called "tit-for-tat" trade war started with China that was misunderstood by many people, in my opinion. I agree that, historically, trade tariffs should be avoided, if possible, but that is assuming that international trade deals are fair and balanced. A major campaign promise made by Trump was that his administration would begin aggressive new trade deal negotiations with our main trading partners, especially China, to be more competitive in the global marketplace, thereby bringing more quality manufacturing jobs back home to America. This policy was never meant to be a long-term economic solution, but rather a short-term bargaining chip to negotiate new trade deals that were more fair and balanced for American businesses. Also, Trump allocated a lot of these new tariff monies to help our farmers who were targeted by the Communist Chinese government. The Chinese were trying to punish American farmers because those in the agricultural industry are strong supporters of Trump. Even though after three years into the Trump administration our overall trade deficits continued to rise, the overall economic statistics during the pre-Covid years were excellent. However, the Democrats won back the majority in the House in the 2018 mid-term elections, with Republicans maintaining their slight majority in the Senate. Tariffs and trade deals were major issues during this campaign, especially in areas that were still struggling to regain those higher-paying manufacturing jobs, and many left-wing pols and media types were still clinging to the now famous "Russia hoax." I remember well the press conference that the president held the day after the mid-term election that he summarized the overall positive results for the Republican Party. Even though Democrats won back a House majority, Republicans won many close elections in non-incumbent races, and did well overall in Senate races to slightly expand their majority. House Majority Leader Paul Ryan and a large number of Republicans retired that year. After a concentrated effort, Republicans failed to "repeal and replace" Obamacare, a major campaign promise. I was very disappointed to watch that final deciding vote cast by powerful Senator John McCain. It was obviously a personal vendetta of McCain's against President Trump when   he uttered on a hot mike, "I'll show Trump how to make America great again" ....then got out of his Senate seat and said in a raised voice, "NO!" I voted for John McCain in 2008, but his action that day was very disheartening to me. I believe he put his own personal feelings ahead of the country's best interests in that moment in history. His decision to vote "no" hurt his party's performance in the mid-term election.

In the winter of 2019, the new Democrat majority in the House certainly made life more   challenging for Trump, especially after Nancy Pelosi became the Speaker of the House again. Other very liberal Democrats, such as Adam Schiff, Jerry Nadler, and Maxine Waters, became committee chairmen and began to control the committee agendas. I will never forget watching these crazy radicals spew their hatred and misinformation about the Russian hoax, advocating for every radical socialist idea under the sun, and call for Trump's impeachment for absolutely no legitimate reason, whatsoever, with no evidence of wrongdoing. Watching their TV clips in the evening was like watching a never-ending bad dream - I suddenly felt I was living in a foreign country. "The Donald" ignored their radical nonsense most of the time and kept working day and night for the "forgotten men and women" of America.

In February, 2019, the president announced that the US was withdrawing from the Intermediate-Range Nuclear Forces Treaty with Russia. Of course, all the liberal Democrats and left-wing media talking heads went nuts again, falsely accusing Trump of wanting a war with Russia, which was the exact opposite of his decision-making thought process. Similar to the Reagan days,

Trump wanted to re- negotiate this treaty from a position of strength, not weakness, and this action also demonstrated that he was not doing Russia and/or Putin any favors, and it made the left-wing Russian hoax narrative appear even more foolish.

The president continued to press on with his popular "America First" agenda, despite having to deal with this new hostile Democrat majority in the House, and even some spineless RINOs (Republicans In Name Only) who were caving in to the left-wing radicals. The economy continued to improve, new trade deals were taking shape, the southern border wall was being built, the military was now better funded and strengthened, and the ISIS terrorist networks were being destroyed. In other words, Trump was keeping his main campaign promises. America was now stronger and more respected around the world.

On June 30, 2019, Trump became the first sitting president to actually step inside the North Korea demilitarized zone when meeting with UN again to ease tensions. Later that year, on October 7, a new trade deal with Japan was signed at the White House and, on October 27, ISIS leader al-Baghdadi was killed in a military raid inside Syria.

Even with this impressive track record of presidential achievements, the insane Democrat House members, on December 18, 2019, passed two articles of impeachment against President Trump based on a routine phone call to the leader of Ukraine. The allegations of abusing his power and obstructing justice were baseless - political rival Joe Biden and his son Hunter were already being publically investigated for THEIR previous abuse of power and unethical behavior during the Obama/Biden years. What I really found outrageous during this time period was that President Trump released the actual word-for-word text of the phone call in question for the press and public to examine, and it was concrete evidence of NO wrongdoing.

Even the leader of Ukraine stated that their phone conversation was very routine and normal. In my opinion, this petty political tactic used by the Democrats was clearly a smokescreen for Joe Biden, because the party establishment wanted him to be the 2020 presidential nominee, and they were alarmed that the extreme Socialist (some would consider Communist) candidate Bernie Sanders was surging ahead in the pre-primary polls. Thankfully, the president was later acquitted of both bogus charges in the US Senate on February 5, 2020. I remember how relieved common-sense conservatives were feeling after this corrupt mess was over; most folks just wanted to return to normal business.

The 2020 Democrat primaries were in full swing now. We enjoyed watching all the TV debates because it was like watching a Saturday Night Live comedy satire. It was a very weak field to start with, "Old Sleepy Joe" was performing very poorly, Bernie Sanders was getting more extreme by the minute, and Senator Liz Warren became the new poster child for the angriest liberal politician in the country. Early in the season, "2% Kamala" Harris accused Biden of being a racial bigot back in the '70s for opposing forced school busing, but it quickly became a moot point when Harris was forced to drop out of the race before the Iowa caucus, due to her whopping 2% approval rating. The other candidates were interesting and gave slick old-school left-wing speeches centered around race, climate change, and how much "free stuff" they wanted to give away which would only worsen the welfare culture (translation: they advocated to raise taxes and waste it on programs that have historically proven to be failures.) It quickly became a primary race between Biden, Warren, and Sanders. The big turning point was when all the candidates rallied behind Biden simply because they thought Sanders was not electable in the fall general election. Poor Bernie got screwed again by the "mean" DNC establishment, and never received even a cabinet appointment after all his time and effort spent.

On March 13, 2020, the historic global tragedy hit. President Trump stated on national live TV that the "invisible enemy" called the "Covid 19" virus was about to reach the shores of America coming from China. He declared a national emergency over the outbreak, and explained to the public several extreme measures that the federal government had planned to implement, including widespread temporary closings of businesses and public facilities. My vivid memory of that news conference is one of shock and concern. Nobody really knew how seriously our lives were going to change, or how long it would last. The stock markets were already crashing around the world that March causing massive and sudden job layoffs. The hospitality industries were especially hit hard as millions of restaurant, bar, and hotel jobs were lost overnight. People were shocked that our wonderfully strong economy was now suddenly in the tank. The school environment was radically changed due to closings and new online classes, and most social events were cancelled. Movie theaters were shut down, online shopping and takeout food became the norm.

The main concern from health experts was that, due to a lack of specific vaccines to fight this unknown virus, extreme measures of social distancing, masking, and sanitizing would be necessary to "control community spread" which would overwhelm medical facilities. In my opinion, President Trump did a very good job of managing this crisis based on the expert advice he was given at the time, but we now know he probably underestimated the total gravity of the crisis, especially how long it would last and the tragically high number of lives that would be lost across the country and the world. He was correct, in my opinion, to keep a laser-beam focus on developing new virus vaccines quickly, and he accomplished this goal through "Operation Warp Speed" in only nine months. A more detailed reflection on the lessons learned from this tragic crisis will be discussed in the next chapter.

When reviewing the actual economic statistics during the first three years of the Trump administration, most objective observers would be impressed. Before Covid hit, unemployment was down to about 3.5%, job openings were up about 20%, we gained about 487,000 manufacturing jobs, and stock market gains made many 401K's and pension plans soar for millions of middle-class workers. The inflation rate was steady at about 5% to 6%, household incomes rose at about 2.5% after inflation, and US crude oil production rose over 36% to keep pump gas prices below $2.00 a gallon, eventually making America "energy independent", a policy that has been proven to maintain national peace and prosperity.

After Covid hit, the unemployment rate suddenly soared by April, 2020, to almost 15% and the Federal Reserve reduced their prime lending rate to almost 0%, which the president and Congress used to borrow about two trillion new dollars to finance a massive emergency Covid relief package. By the November, 2020, election, unemployment dropped back down to about 6.7%. My wife and I certainly felt this economic pain as the promotional products industry lost a lot of routine business during this time period because of many cancelled special events, trade shows, concerts, and business conferences. Even the larger corporate and non-profit clients that had substantial marketing/advertising budgets simply were not placing orders; they suddenly went into "shutdown mode" and did not have any clue when things would be back to "normal." However, the promo industry got creative quickly to cope with the business and health crisis as suddenly factories were producing custom-imprinted logo masks, hand sanitizers, and social distancing signs/decals to regain some lost business. We also started having tenants in our rental properties struggling to pay their rent due to sudden job layoffs. There were new Covid rent relief federal monies that were available, but we discovered that the state and local governments were having trouble dispersing those funds to families who really needed help. Even with good intentions, the feds grossly underestimated the bureaucratic capacities of local governments to release these relief monies, especially considering worker shortages that added to the challenge. After the vaccines became widely available, business conditions began to improve. My wife and I made the decision to receive our vaccine shots and experienced no major side effects.

The final few months of the Trump presidency were very disappointing to us to say the least. The Chinese virus continued to drag on with no end in sight, the reality of a new recession was sinking in even when business started to improve, and the summer urban riots spurred by BLM of 2020 seemed totally unjustified. It became obvious to me as I watched in horror as major urban areas were being burned down and looted, that big city mayors and city councils were not only tolerating this absurd violence, they were actually advocating this criminal behavior! While Democrat nominee Joe Biden was hiding in his Delaware basement (instead of campaigning around the country like a normal candidate), his VP running mate "2% Kamala" was raising jail bail money for these violent criminals. TV reporters broadcasted all these "peaceful protests" while we saw burning cars and buildings in the background! These riots started after the controversial George Floyd tragedy in Minneapolis, and I understood the strong emotions at the time. Nobody thinks abuse of power is ever justified, but widespread urban violence is never the answer to these problems. Surely most common-sense Americans agree that "defund the police" policies will never improve our justice system, it will only increase crime and violence and destroy the moral fabric of our society! Frankly, I thought President Trump should have been more aggressive in the use of federal troops and the federalizing of local National Guard personnel to better control these violent urban riots.

As the riots dragged on late in the summer and early fall of 2020, it became obvious to me that these criminal actions had

NOTHING to do with George Floyd, and everything to do with the organized chaos of the left-wing front groups who just wanted Trump to appear bad in the eyes of the voting public. Once again, our corrupt and biased left-wing mass media were more than happy to facilitate this   goal.

When the fall, 2020, election rolled around, I still thought that President Trump would win re-election, based on his overall positive first term performance. Even after he was infected with Covid that October, he bounced back in just a few days and campaigned like a young man drawing huge rally crowds, in stark contrast to Biden's lethargic basement campaign. Election night was a huge disappointment for us as, suddenly, just when it appeared that Trump had a second term in the bag, vote counting stopped in the key swing states! What the hell was going on? It took another few days to actually count these votes from millions of Covid-related mail-in ballots to then declare Biden the winner!

This decision remains very controversial and upsetting to many conservative Trump supporters, and evidence is still coming in that documents widespread voting irregularities within these six key swing states that decided the election. One thing is certain beyond a shadow of a doubt: when millions of dedicated registered voters believe that a presidential election was not held in a fair and honest manner, our sacred democracy is in trouble! We MUST find all the answers to move forward as a united people, and these documented answers MUST become transparent!

Due to this controversial election outcome, thousands of peaceful Trump protesters came to the US Capitol on January 6, 2021, the day Congress was to formally certify the election results. My wife has personal friends that actually participated in this mainly peaceful protest, and they told her that no actual Trump supporters were involved in the rioting and illegal entering of the Capitol building. The chaos that ensued was obviously another radical left-wing setup job against Trump as he was leaving office, and gave the radical Democrats one last excuse to impeach Trump again on bogus charges to keep him from running again in 2024. The corrupt House again pushed through another impeachment vote, but the Senate wisely again acquitted the president of any wrongdoing. The real crime committed that sad day was the unlawful murder of unarmed protester Ashley Babbitt by a Capitol police officer, and the total failure of Nancy Pelosi to maintain proper peace and security in the first place.

The ongoing failures of the new Biden administration will be discussed in the closing chapters.

I cannot ever remember a PERFECT America,

but I do remember a BETTER America!

CHAPTER 9

Mistakes Learned From the Political Correctness and Covid Eras

In recent years, America and even the world has suffered from the hyper-sensitive nonsense known as "political correctness (PC)." I first noticed this movement as a young city councilman back in the late 1980s and early 1990s during routine meetings and community gatherings. A local citizen uttered the innocent term "Mr. Chairman" before another community activist shouted out, "You mean chair-person, don't you?" I thought to myself that was pretty silly, but I also was raised to respect everyone's civil/equal rights by my decent "greatest generation" parents. Later, the elected term "alderman" changed to "alderwoman" if that city council member happened to be a female, and recently the elected term of alderman has officially changed to "city council member." When left-wing historians make a point that our sacred documents should change famous statements such as "all men are created equal" to "all men and women are created equal", or change "all men" to "all humankind", etc., that really doesn't bother me, per se, but these hair-splitting demands are more than meets the eye. Where does this stuff come from? When our citizens are afraid to utter the wrong word, the wrong phase, or to simply use an innocent traditional name such as a sports team's mascot (such as the Arkansas State University Indians) without offending someone or some group, it contradicts our precious First Amendment rights of free speech, free religion, free press, and freedoms of assembly. When we review the origins and the more absurd examples of political correctness, every freedom-loving American should be concerned, or even alarmed, regarding the long-term damage it has done to our country!

No one ever wants to be viewed as insensitive, sexist, racist, or offensive in any way, especially appearing in any way that could affect their professional reputation or job status in a negative manner. Unfortunately, that is exactly what has been happening to hard-working and well-intentioned citizens for many years now. When I was younger, a lot of these politically correct examples seemed so strange and petty that many folks just thought they were amusing. Ignoring the source of the complaint and moving on with their daily lives was the norm. But things are not at all amusing anymore - these events have become very serious.

The PC culture (derived from the serious and harmful political ideology of Marxism many years ago) started to become "hip" during the radical college protests during the 1960s' anti-Vietnam War era. The modern PC culture is clearly a "totalitarian" political ideology because it artificially creates "victim groups" based on race, gender, social/economic class, etc. to justify radical and sometimes illegal actions. The disgusting urban riots during the summer of 2020 were a classic example of this injustice.

We must return to the fundamental policies of law and order to save our country. Economic Marxism states that our history has been determined by private ownership of property and worker production, but the modern PC mobs promote that all of history should be determined by raw power, and nothing else matters. Translation: this warped sense of justice attempts to justify criminal behavior such as the urban burning, looting, and violence that we witnessed, all in the name of "racial and social justice."

This politically correct culture is dangerous because they tend to label automatically certain minority groups such as African-American, Hispanic, Gay, Feminists, etc., as "good" because they are considered to be the "victims" of society, and they label other groups such as business owners and police officers as "bad" because they are considered the "oppressors," regardless of their behavior or actions. This brand of stereotyping is not only inaccurate and unfair, it is a certain recipe for social chaos.

Marxist PC logic is also used to wrongly justify preferential treatment of the so-called "oppressed" groups that can be easily documented at colleges and universities, and the business communities in recent years. These "affirmative action" programs are a classic example of this injustice. Most conservatives view these policies as nothing short of reverse discrimination. The evil Marxist PC culture is a method that automatically gives these radical groups the answers that they want to justify their misguided behavior. It is used as an excuse to rewrite our history and always puts America in a negative light - keeping these groups in their "victim" status, which demands more and more government assistance and dependency. Moreover, make no mistake about it, these radical actions are not an accident, they are very much by design. They are very much intended to "transform America" in a very bad way. The overall intent is to bring our country closer and closer toward a Socialist/Communist totalitarian government. We must move forward NOW to end these very destructive political, social, and cultural practices to truly "Make America Great Again!"

In order to appreciate the seriousness of this PC culture, I believe it is important to review   some of the commonly used terms that I consider to be nonsense, and explore a few of the classical examples of the destructive power of the PC culture. I ran across over one hundred commonly used PC terms, but here are a few of my favorites that might make you laugh (or cry):

1. Illegal immigrant is now "irregular immigrant" or "undocumented worker" (an Obama favorite)

2. Right-wing protest is now "a riot" (a favorite of the mass media)

3. Left-wing riot is now "a protest" (another mass media favorite)

4. Terrorist is now a "freedom fighter/rebel/ protester/ insurgent" (another Obama favorite)

5. Global warming is now "climate change" (the entire Democrat Party promotes this scam)

6. Criminals are now "behaviorally challenged" (liberals love this one)

7. Natural disaster is now a "global warming incident" (Biden pitched this one recently)

8. Preferential treatment is now "Affirmative Action" (code name = reverse discrimination)

9. Racist is now "someone who disagrees with the far-left" (BLM favorite)

10. Nazi is now "someone who disagrees with the far-left" (Crazy Maxine Waters' favorite)

11. Fascist is now "someone who disagrees with the far-left" (college campus favorite)

12. Merry Christmas is now "season's greetings"/ "happy holidays" (large companies love this one)

13. Illegal Voter is now "undocumented voter" (a DNC favorite)

14. Illegal aliens are now "undocumented migrants" ("2% Kamala" loves this one)

To illustrate how the PC culture can have deadly consequences, the tragic incident at a Texas US Army base in 2009 should bring chill bumps up your spine. Army Psychologist Nidal Malik Hasan killed 13 people as he opened gun fire while shouting "God is Great" in Arabic. The Pentagon, during the Obama administration, knew about Hasan's emails that promoted radical Islam and unusual policy recommendations for other Muslims serving in the military. Other personnel referred to him as a "ticking time bomb," but these warnings were ignored. The Army's middle-management folks ignored these warnings because they were "afraid to be accused of profiling somebody."

Recently, administrators at a California high school sent five students home after they refused to remove their American flag t-shirts on Cinco de Mayo Day (Mexican Day of Independence.) One of the boys stated to a TV reporter that the administrator told them they could wear their US flag shirts any other day, but it was a "little insensitive" to wear an American flag shirt on this Mexican holiday. The school Superintendent later described the incident "as extremely unfortunate" and said the incident would be investigated further. As a former public educator, this action was simply wrong. You should never instruct any student to change clothes unless the clothing worn is a direct violation of the student handbook.

In 2003, the director of the LA County affirmative action office issued a memo that ordered a detailed search for any computer equipment labeled "master" and "slave." These traditional computer names for computer hardware were deemed "unacceptable and offensive," and they requested that all suppliers stop using these labels. After one worker noticed a videotape machine bearing these long-standing industry terms, he filed a discrimination complaint with the office compliance people. Due to overwhelming negative publicity and counter-complaints from suppliers, the purchasing manager promised there would not be any future bans on computer equipment with the traditional labels.

Conservatives were appalled watching the mean-spirited US Senate circus-like atmosphere during the confirmation of Supreme Court nominee Brett Kavanagh in 2018. It was a stark and tragic example of political correctness as Judge Kavanagh was blindsided with totally false accusations of inappropriate behavior during his high school years -yes, high school years! As I reflect upon those surreal TV Senate hearings, it was beyond shocking - it was downright painful to see this man being crucified in front of the country, with his wife and kids by his side. With ZERO factual evidence, these accusations were being broadcast on national TV for days and weeks. The worst thing to watch was how many Democrat senators participated in this white-collar lynching, making dramatic accusations with no direct evidence. Our sacred Constitutional principles of "due process" and the rule of law were being totally ignored; suddenly we were watching the "guilty until proven innocent" show, and these arrogant left-wingers were in a panic to deny President Trump and a highly qualified judge this Supreme Court seat. The Democrats let it slip, in another stereotype, that because Judge Kavanagh happened to be of the Catholic faith, he would automatically vote against any current or future abortion rights legislation, even after he testified that he considered the famous Roe vs. Wade case law as "settled law." As these hearings dragged on, it became more and more obvious what the Democratic goal was - to block Kavanagh's confirmation by any means needed, regardless how mean-spirited, false, and ludicrous the accusations became. The Democrats kept promoting the theory of "victimhood" - that we should always believe any accusation of inappropriate behavior at face value, especially if the accusation is made by a female, even if the facts and evidence of wrongdoing are suspect. As this sad chapter in American politics was winding down, Republican Senator Lindsey Graham came to the defense of Judge Kavanagh and reminded his judiciary committee peers that the whole process of this specific confirmation hearing had been grossly unfair in every respect….a character assassination of a very decent and qualified judge based on ZERO evidence and wild hearsay, ignoring our precious rule of law. This was Senator Graham's finest moment of his long career, in my opinion. Finally Judge Kavanagh was confirmed, because the overall public sentiment was in his favor. Most Americans strongly believe in our Constitutional principles of due process and the rule of law.

A recent study was conducted by the "More in Common" international organization to better understand how Americans view political correctness. After interviewing over 8,000 respondents around the country, about 80% of these Americans oppose political correctness and believe that it is "a problem in our country." Also, their views of PC were overwhelmingly unfavorable among all subgroups (liberal, moderate, conservative, etc.), EXCEPT for within the 8% of the country that falls into the "progressive activist" category. Within this progressive subgroup, only about 30% interviewed the PC culture as a problem. It appears to me and most folks around the country that the recent PC culture certainly is not mainstream, even among the "classical liberals" who still believe in our civil liberties and the rule of law. The Kavanagh victory and other political victories that put traditional principles and common sense ahead of mob PC hysteria are not only a win for conservatives, they are a win for all civilized society.

The bottom line is that political correctness is a very serious problem in our country these days and we must take steps now to correct this "cancel culture" before our nation is destroyed from within. What many of the left-wingers consider just "insensitive" language and/or actions by people that believe in traditional American values runs much deeper…it is a serious and historical political ideology that originated from the father of communism, and it is meant to control our sacred freedoms and to lead our wonderful country down the path of destruction and negativity. We CAN and MUST stop these deceptive forces before they destroy the moral fiber of our democratic republic!

As we all begin to reflect upon the tragic Covid-19 era that started in late 2019 in Wuhan, China, to me, personally, it still seems like a bad dream. I never thought I would live long enough to witness such a horrible global pandemic that has affected millions of people in such a negative way. I vividly remember in January, 2020, watching that first press conference when President Trump announced a public health emergency, and our own US Senator Tom Cotton from Arkansas encouraged the president to immediately restrict air flights from China to help control the spread of the disease. When President Trump declared a "national emergency" on March 13, 2020, I realized AT THAT MOMENT that America and the entire world was headed into dark historic days. Frankly, a lot of the science involving this horrible virus was over my head at the time, and I must admit that I never envisioned how much damage Covid would bring. I believe our leaders and "health experts" were somewhat surprised, too, how long it has lingered throughout our world. I still believe that the Trump administration did a decent job of governing through the early periods of the health crisis, based on the health/scientific knowledge and advice given at the time.

Clearly we know now that mistakes were made. In my opinion, Trump's main mistakes were that he underestimated the widespread health and long-term economic damage the virus would cause, and maybe gave advisors Dr. Fauci and Dr. Burks too much power early in the pandemic. They were both wrong about several aspects of the crisis. We now know that the severe "economic lockdowns" and health mandates spear-headed by the more liberal Democrat governors and mayors around the country were extreme, and that the Covid crisis was used as a political weapon to harm Trump heading into the 2020 presidential election.

One of the main positive accomplishments of the Trump administration was that his policies greatly improved the national economy. Employment was historically low, inflation was kept in check, interest rates were low, and new fairer trade deals were taking hold. The Democrats did everything in their power to weaken the economy during the 2020 Covid period for one simple reason: to hurt President Trump's chances of obtaining re-election. The big Democrat push for unprecedented mail-in voting ballots was nothing more than a scam and the health-related voting procedures were simply a false narrative, all to hurt Trump and having nothing to do with public health and safety.

In all fairness, the national GOP made their share of political mistakes during the Covid voting season as well. They did fight against the shady massive mail-in ballot systems, but once they lost that battle to a Democrat-controlled Congress, they should have prepared better to deal with this new campaign reality. The main six important "swing states" that decided the presidential election were poorly managed by mainly Republican-controlled state legislatures and Secretaries of State, especially in Georgia. President Trump did a great job in spearheading "Operation Warped Speed" that developed the first Covid vaccines in only about nine months. I was personally disappointed that this positive news wasn't announced until after the election - it could have helped Trump immensely, in my opinion. He did a wonderful job helping the hard-hit areas of New York and Los Angeles by sending huge floating hospital ships that were underutilized, and by obtaining critical supplies such as ventilators, masks, gloves, etc., very quickly by invoking the Defense Production Act of 1950.

It also now appears that our health experts may have underestimated how fast the Covid virus would mutate into the different "variants" that made the spread of the disease more difficult to control. It seemed like every time we were about to defeat the virus spread, another variant would suddenly be created, causing a new and different challenge. Most people I know believed in taking the basic prudent precautions such as getting vaccinated, masking in close environments, social distancing, hand sanitizing, etc., but I believe most people now realize that our society went overboard when school districts continued to lock down public schools for extended periods of time, even after most people were vaccinated. Our children did not benefit from this decision. We now know that many urban areas enacted excessive lockdown mandates that made no health sense, but it did do permanent damage to many small businesses. My wife and I certainly felt this economic slowdown within both the promotional products and rental business communities.

As we continue to reflect upon this very difficult time in our history, let us never forget the most important lesson that we have learned: the human cost of this tragic era. America has recorded over one million deaths due to Covid-19 and my beloved

Arkansas lost over 11,000 citizens due to this horrible disease in just over two years. We personally lost around a dozen friends to Covid, including our favorite FedEx delivery man. One of my old high school friends lost her 29-year-old son-in-law, leaving behind his young wife and three kids, and my wife lost her very sweet 54-year-old female cousin in October, 2021.

We must never forget the extreme sacrifices of our front-line health workers that have been over-worked and over-stressed trying to save lives. We must never forget the beloved family members and friends that have been very ill and those who died from this horrible disease, especially the younger mothers and fathers that will never see their kids grow up. We must never forget the dedicated scientists and researchers that have worked endless hours to develop the new vaccines and medicines to keep our country healthy and happy. We should never forget that we CAN and MUST be better prepared for the next health crisis and that we should share our new health discoveries with the world when possible for the sake of humanity. And, yes, the United States of America should lead the world and be the shining example of quality healthcare, especially during a global health crisis. In the future, our American leaders should not depend on the advice from the World Health Organization (WHO). We now know there is substantial evidence that the WHO displayed bias in favor of China regarding the origins and spread of Covid early in the pandemic, and very likely under-reported Covid-related deaths within Communist China.

I cannot ever remember a PERFECT America,

but I do remember a BETTER America!

CHAPTER 10

Boomer Reflections and Traditional American Values Create HOPE for the Future

The national nightmare of the Biden-Harris administration started on January 20, 2021. The controversial presidential election of 2020 and the ethical fallout afterward was upsetting to me, but watching Joe Biden and Kamala Harris take the inaugural reins of power on live TV was painful.   My first thought was that these individuals were not ready to lead this great country and, to date, they have proven me right, unfortunately. On his first full day as president, Biden signed 17 executive orders intended for a single purpose: to undo President

Donald Trump's legacy of "common sense populism" that made America great again. Biden's first actions as president included halting the southern border wall funding, reversing the travel bans from Muslim-dominated countries, reinstating the ill-advised agreements with the World Health Organization and the expensive Paris Climate Change accords. Every one of these presidential orders have been proven failures, and they continue to cause a general decline in our country.

Clearly, any objective observer would agree that President Biden and VP Harris have failed to provide competent leadership to date. They failed to defeat the Covid crisis in a timely manner, and they have not even discussed ideas to hold the communist Chinese government accountable for starting the global pandemic. Our southern border that was secure during the Trump years is now totally out of control. "2% Kamala" has been a miserable failure as the new "border czar." Inflation has continued to soar upward, especially for gas/diesel and food products.

It reminds me a lot of the Jimmy Carter years as president when I was a student in college. Those Carter years were especially tough times for young people because of the same failed Democrat policies (high inflation, high interest rates and a chaotic and weak foreign policy), except that the current Biden administration policies are even more extreme and hurtful to the country.

The botched military and refugee withdrawals from Afghanistan were also painful to watch. This chaos reminded me of the final fall of Saigon at the end of the Vietnam War in 1975 when I was about to graduate from high school. In addition to leaving billions of dollars of valuable military equipment for the Taliban terrorists to use against us down the road, America has lost the respect and admiration that was accomplished during the Trump administration. Our allies no longer trust us and our enemies no longer fear us. I am confident that Russia would never have invaded Ukraine if Donald J. Trump was still our Commander-In-Chief. While thousands of innocent citizens have been slaughtered in Ukraine, an incompetent President Biden and a weak NATO alliance have remained on the sidelines, demonstrating their lack of courage and leadership. These brutal "crimes against humanity" led by Dictator Putin are among the worst in the history of the world, and the weak response from the

West has been inadequate…too little, too late. Once again, peace through strength is the only proper answer.

When the Russian's invasion of Ukraine began in February, 2022, the TV images of the Russian bombing and shelling of Ukraine ordered by the ruthless dictator Vladimir Putin were painful to watch. This communist act of military aggression was totally unjustified and certainly contradicted international law. The sad images of innocent civilians fleeing their once-free country reminded me of those old World War II films of Adolph Hitler's crimes against humanity in Europe during the late 1930s and early 1940s. In my opinion, President Biden once again demonstrated weak and ineffective leadership during the weeks leading up to the Russian invasion of Ukraine. Even though I totally agreed that we wanted to avoid another world war, we should have invoked tougher military and economic sanctions earlier to discourage Putin from using military force against Ukraine. It was obvious that Putin was an evil thug dictator who was trying to force the spread of Communism and gain more land territory by any means necessary, regardless of the human pain and suffering it caused. The Russian propaganda of wanting a nearby "neutral territory" that is outside the NATO alliance for peace and stability was utter nonsense. Putin was acting just like Hitler during the early days of World War II, and we should always remember that evil dictators simply MUST be stopped. If they are not promptly defeated, they will continue their evil tyranny.

After enduring the first painful year of the Biden/Harris administration, my wife and I were still   hoping that common sense would eventually prevail and some positive change would begin to occur, but we have not seen that change to date. On March 1, 2022, we did our patriotic duty and watched President Biden's first official "State of the Union" address to a joint session of Congress, sincerely hoping that we would hear a positive reversal of his failed left-wing policies. He did demonstrate more overall energy and enthusiasm during the speech than usual, but we remained disappointed that he basically   tried to "resell" the public on his already failed big government and "build back better" proposals. We agreed in principal with his opening remarks supporting Ukraine's efforts to fight back the unjustified Russian military aggression, but we were disappointed that he didn't offer more help with actual military weapons that could win their long-term freedom and security. Also, many of his speech details were simply not true and/or were exaggerated; our southern border was NOT secure, our national economy was NOT stronger, rising inflation had NOT been temporary, we had NOT defeated the Covid pandemic, our global image had NOT improved, and the climate-change policies should NOT have been a top priority for our country. Biden also missed a golden opportunity during this speech….he should have announced that we would return to the Trump-era policies of being "energy independent" by cranking up domestic oil and gas production and stop importing ANY oil products from ANY country, especially communist countries. Our president instead doubled-down on his climate change agenda to appease the radical left wing of the Democrat Party, at the same time that thousands of innocent Ukrainian freedom-loving citizens were being slaughtered by an evil power-hungry dictator.

My friends, this mindset is the epitome of FAILED LEADERSHIP, and it creates a more dangerous world for us all!

In all fairness, the president did surprise us with some positive news. He finally stated that we   should "fund the police," not "defund the police," as stated by the mobs during the 2020 urban riots that were supported by "2% Kamala" and liberal Democrat mayors across the country. Hopefully, Biden will support more police funding for the correct resources, such as more modern equipment, more qualified trained police officers, more high-tech police vehicles and training, etc. If he means to better fund police for more critical race theory brainwashing-type training, then he is simply wrong again, and conservatives need to promptly defeat those proposals through their local city councils and mayoral networks.

Even though President Biden tried to reassure the American people that the national economy was rapidly improving during his speech, high inflation and rising interest rates continued to rage on during the summer and fall of 2022. Republicans continued to argue that the Biden and Democrat economic policies were not working for the average hard-working American leading up to the 2022 mid- term elections, and many conservatives blamed Biden's weak foreign policies on the horrible Russian military invasion of Ukraine, especially after several multi-billion dollar aid packages were sent with no end or exit strategy in sight.

On June 24, 2022, a shocking historic event occurred out of the blue that greatly upset liberal Democrats. The landmark

Supreme Court decision of "Roe vs. Wade" that legalized abortions in 1973 was overturned by the more conservative Supreme Court that was created by former President Trump's three justice appointments. The more liberal Democrat groups in the country were surprised and outraged, and prompted national protests…even protesting outside several of the conservative justices' private residences in a mean-spirited and threatening tone. I was personally disgusted when I later viewed Democrat Senate majority leader Chuck Schumer on TV stating in front of an angry mob of protesters: "We are going to get you for this, Kavanaugh!" It sounded like the leader of the United States Senate just publicly threatened a United States Supreme Court justice for doing his sworn duty and rendering his sincere legal opinion on a very important social and health issue that affects millions of innocent unborn American children. More conservative Republican groups responded by stating that Roe and the Casey court case decisions do not "outlaw" abortions, per se, but merely mandate that that the individual state governments must now decide how to regulate abortion procedures in the future. Several conservative "red" states, such as Arkansas, swiftly began to enact stricter abortion laws, and several more liberal "blue" states, such as New York, promptly declared that abortions will remain "safe and legal" within their borders.

Later, in the summer of 2022, more political drama began to unfold. In another surprise development of the over-reaching Biden administration, the FBI suddenly conducted a "search raid" of former President Trump's private residence known as "Mar-A-Lago" in Palm Beach, Florida, on August 24, 2022. They stated to Trump's attorneys that they were searching for missing "classified documents" that Trump allegedly refused to submit to the National Archives officials before leaving office in January, 2021. Trump argued that these documents were "declassified" while he had the presidential power to do so, and posed no threats to national security. Of course, the mass media and the Democrats tried to capitalize on this, in conjunction with their never-ending "we hate Trump" witch hunts. Even several liberal legal scholars disagreed with this unprecedented governmental over-reach of a former U.S. president and thought this aggressive action ordered by the federal DOJ was a violation of Trump's civil liberties, not to mention a waste of taxpayers' money. In sharp contrast, the recent discoveries of classified documents found in President Biden's offices and private residences do suggest possible legal and national security problems because Biden was a sitting vice president during these document time periods and vice presidents do NOT have the legal authority to declassify any materials. Moreover, Republicans have recently suggested that these classified documents may be directly connected to various foreign "influence peddling" activities while Biden was vice president…and, even worse, may be connected to his son's (Hunter Biden's) "laptop from hell" computer that documents his graphic drug use and illegal prostitution activities. This computer material also documents many personal emails sent to business partners describing elaborate international money-making schemes involving millions of dollars during Biden's years as vice president, especially unusual and very lucrative "consulting" activities in China and Ukraine. One email even eludes to then-Vice President Biden as "the big guy." Several Republicans claim that this email may be the "smoking gun" of guilt that directly connects the "Biden crime family" to illegal international crime activities and may even lead to President Biden's eventual resignation or House impeachment. Only time will tell.

Leading up to the November, 2022, mid-term elections, political excitement was in the air, especially for conservatives eager to make changes to our recent extreme left-wing members of Congress and, hopefully, even to elect a few new conservative governors around the country. Conservative groups and media outlets were predicting a "big red wave" due to the widespread anger over the failures of radical Democratic policies. High inflation, rising interest rates, insane open border policies, the war in Ukraine, the crazy "green new deal," and political correctness/cancel culture-gone-wild seemed like a historic recipe for disaster for the Democrats. In reality, the "big red wave" transpired into the "small red ripple," which was a devastating disappointment to Republicans. After the dust settled, it appeared that, once again, the Democrats performed a much better election strategy with mail-in balloting, early voting drives, strong fundraising, and probably better overall candidate "ground-game" campaigning. Republicans lost many close elections they should have won, and it became obvious that their overall national campaign strategy and organization was somewhat flawed. However, they were able to win a narrow Republican majority in the U.S. House which was certainly a game changer for at least 2023 and 2024 and maybe beyond. Moderate Representative Kevin McCarthy from California was elected as the new Speaker of the House after 15 rounds of balloting from his colleagues, but he had to make several concessions with the more conservative "Freedom Caucus" led by Representative Jim Jordan from Ohio. McCarthy conceded to several rule changes, specific committee assignments, and made promises to negotiate major spending budget cuts with President Biden to secure the needed votes. Controlling the agenda via House committee chairs gives conservatives substantially more power and that is a good thing for America. However, the Democrats were able to hold on to a slight majority in the U.S. Senate (51 to 49) after Hershel Walker's narrow defeat in the Georgia Senate run-off election.

Shortly after the mid-term elections, on November 15, 2022, former President Trump announced that he was indeed planning to run a third presidential campaign. His conservative "America First" voter base celebrated this news, and I was one of those voters that celebrated, as well! In my opinion, any objective comparisons between the Trump and Biden administrations would conclude that the average American worker was much better off during the Trump years, with maybe the exception being during the peak of the Covid pandemic which was certainly not the fault of President Trump. Even   if you don't personally "like" Donald J. Trump, the cold hard economic and social facts document that a conservative "common sense" populist leader led America back to greatness. Even if you personally "like" President Biden (and even wish him success), the opposite objective conclusion is clearly that Joe Biden has basically failed to lead America in a positive direction, at least to date. The reasons are quite simple: after over 50 years in public service, he has sold his soul out to a small group of far-left extremists that promote the international SCAM called "climate change" which has nothing to do with a clean environment and everything to do with money, power, and global CONTROL over your everyday lives. Biden has sold out to the radical global socialist elites (some would argue "global communists") that don't believe in putting "America First" – they believe in putting America LAST. They actually believe that they are smarter than you, more distinguished than you, more righteous than you and, therefore, they believe that they are more entitled than you. These elites believe that America was founded on a sinful premise of slavery and racist oppression;

they believe that our founding fathers were evil people, and they believe that America should promote a global society of "borderless" countries and donate an endless stream of financial welfare to foreign countries, and they will continue to deliver Obama-like speeches that apologize for the American principles of "exceptionalism" that make our country the greatest nation in world history.

Clearly, I REJECT these notions! I believe that the United States of America is, without a doubt, the greatest country that world civilization has ever known, that we have always been a noble people who cherish freedom, civil liberties, and truth and justice. Our democratic republic has survived for over 250 years because we have a government that has maintained checks and balances of power - far from perfect, but it has been functional most of the time. Most of us believe in "peace through strength," and that the sacred right to own and bear arms has kept us free from total governmental tyranny over these many years. We believe in regular free and fair elections within every level of government to hold the people in power accountable...for the people and by the people. Many of us, including myself, believe that the founding and development of America was no accident, rather it was truly by divine providence that led our ancestors to this great land. There are simply too many beautiful natural blessings bestowed upon us to be anything accidental! God bless America!!

As I now view the world through the lens of a highly educated mature senior citizen, I am frankly amazed at how predictable certain news events and social changes have become. And as I grow older, it amazes me how smart and decent our American ancestors were, especially my parents and grand-parents. Yes, history tends to repeat itself, both the good and the bad, and I believe it is important to reflect upon these world and national events and learn from them.

It is my strong belief that we as a society have lost our way in many respects in recent years. Many of us have forgotten how important our traditional American values have been in creating the wealthiest country world civilization has ever known - not only our material/financial wealth, but our spiritual wealth as well. Real Americans believe in broad freedoms, equal opportunity, "rugged individualism," and fair competition. They believe in solid family values, self-government, democracy, hard work, and equal justice for all. We should all embrace the sacred principles of our founding fathers that were articulated so brilliantly through the United States Constitution, Bill of Rights, and Declaration of Independence. We should be role models of American patriots for our children and grandchildren. We should always exercise our sacred right to vote in every election: national, state, and local. We should never be afraid to speak out against governmental or social tyranny. We should stay involved in our local community, especially in anything that affects our children's quality of education. We should always strive for American excellence in all our endeavors, professionally and personally, and teach our children to do the same, including helping others to achieve along the way.

After 65 years of living and learning on this wonderful earth, I clearly do not have all the answers to life - but I DO know certain things are true: FREEDOM WORKS, Socialism and Communism do NOT! Over the years, I have seen many political/social proposals succeed and fail, even when presented with noble intentions.

Here are my proposals for a "Better America".....

THE MCDONALD PLAN

- **Support the current "Convention of the States"** movement that will enact **Article 5** of the US Constitution, which will mandate congressional term limits, a federal balanced budget Amendment, and will return considerable federal powers back to state and local governments, discovering new ways to reduce the size, complexity, costs, and power of federal bureaucracies. (See website for more information: **www.conventionofstates.com**)

- **Support any other legal mechanisms that will mandate reasonable term limits for ALL elected political office holders** at every level of government: national, state, county, and local.

- **Elect TRUE conservatives** (no RINOs or fake conservatives) to every elected office possible.

- **Abolish mail-in ballots/drop boxes and early voting periods** for all national, state and local elections, except for military personnel on active duty serving out of the country. All elections should be subject to professional and independent audits to ensure election integrity, and these findings should be made public in a very timely manner. All final election results should be completed on election night, if possible.

- **Secure our national borders at once,** finish the southern border wall, fund the border patrol with the latest and best personnel & equipment, implement E-verify, abolish out-of-date DACA program, but pass comprehensive immigration reform.

- **Increase police and national defense funding** for proven practical "best practices" and equipment.

- **Cut wasteful spending in social and welfare programs** that have proven to be failures since the 1960s' "Great Society" programs.

- **Return excellent patriotic and social values** to our public school systems. Abolish the federal department of education and return local control of our public schools, allow for daily morning period for voluntary student silent prayer and Bible reading time (constitutional).

- **Abolish the Federal Internal Revenue Service (IRS) and Environmental Protection Agency (EPA)** in the current forms. True conservatives in Congress should greatly reduce and simplify these overly zealous agencies. Federal tax collections and paperwork could be greatly reduced by eliminating loopholes and implementing "flat tax" rates for most Americans. Most EPA regulatory powers should be shifted to state and local governments. The expensive and non-practical "climate change" regulations should be eliminated. Both agencies' "police powers" should be greatly reduced, in accordance with the U.S. Constitution.

- **Abolish all federal "death/estate/inheritance" taxes,** especially for American family farms, ranches and small businesses. Most "capital gains" taxes should be reduced to zero (0%). We need to stop punishing the people that achieve business success that keep out economy strong and vibrant. It is always better to create jobs than welfare checks.

- **Teach American patriotic studies and good citizenship practices** (no politically correct re-writing of history allowed) in every school in the United States, starting by requiring daily morning reciting of the "Pledge of Allegiance" with a crisp US flag in every classroom. Abolish the teaching of "critical race theory" that promotes the false narrative of a racist America.

- **State and local governments should provide incentives to young people** to increase practical vocational/technical training that coincides with the careers that are in the highest demand of the real-world job market, providing the highest income and benefits possible. Conversely, these reforms should reduce the costly and wasteful time spent on non-practical liberal arts education that provides fewer decent jobs, and creates many high student debt problems.

- **Elect leaders that will make America "energy independent" again.** Our domestic oil and gas production should be increased to FULL capacity, prohibit ANY importing of oil/gas products. Alternative energy sources such as solar, wind, and hydro are also useful, but these sources alone cannot provide the energy that America needs. We MUST produce our fossil fuels at FULL capacity to keep our country strong, secure, and independent!

- **Encourage more volunteer community involvement and discourage government dependency**. Promote traditional American values, especially by improving the structure of the nuclear family. Our compassionate country should always ensure a basic "safety net" for our people who truly need   help, especially our brave wounded warriors that have made great sacrifices to secure our freedom. But we need to accept that the "welfare culture" that left-wing politicians created back in the 1960s   has been **a tragic failure,** and we should do everything in our power to discourage the long-term dependency on the government.

- **Congress should immediately conduct a comprehensive review of all imported products** that could   potentially reduce our national security during a time of conflict, especially from communist countries. Products such as pharmaceuticals, high-tech items, and scarce raw materials needed for energy and/or defense products, should be identified now to facilitate new domestic manufacturing.

- **Conservative patriots should declare a non-violent war on the current "cancel culture"** that has been promoted by radical PC activists that make up a small and mean-spirited minority group of our society. As a reminder, these radicals are out of touch with any common-sense realities of modern and civilized society, and their violent disrespectful behavior should simply be rejected.

  Peaceful protest is their American right, I have no problem with any group that wants to express their opinion, but when they start breaking our laws and become violent, they need to be arrested and punished for their unlawful actions. Elect more conservative mayors and city council members if you want to return to decent urban law and order.

- **Forbid any male athlete to participate in female sports.** The current trend is simply wrong and unfair. And, of course, no male person in this country should ever be allowed inside a female restroom and/or dressing room facility. I have always supported basic equality, but this practice is an insult to our intelligence!

In conclusion, America must return to the Judeo-Christian values that our founding fathers promoted and discussed in the original sacred documents. Of course, they were not perfect, they were just men who yearned for their God-given "natural rights" of freedom and opportunity. They had an amazing vision for the future of the United States of America, and they made great sacrifices to secure that vision. Our modern society should embrace their principles of courage and optimism, and we should all be reminded that these past achievements did not happen by accident.

There is no substitute for the American work ethic and the drive for excellence. There is no substitute for truth and justice, and there is no replacement for basic integrity and human dignity. Our American ancestors knew that no government would be "perfect," but they also knew that a nation that provides broad freedoms and liberties within a structured governmental system of "checks and balances" had the best chance for long-term survival....and they were right! They also knew that past governments that promoted a totalitarian type system with limited liberties usually failed, or at least did not provide a decent life for their citizens...in other words, they knew that governments that promoted big centralized forms of control was not good. Even a young nation that experienced obvious injustices such as slavery, gender/class discrimination, regional inequalities, etc., created a system that allowed those injustices to be corrected by and for the people.

Even with all our current problems, **we MUST move forward with the "miracle of America"** that our ancestors started for us. We MUST continue to learn from our past, our victories and failures, our injustices and the correction of those injustices, our future new ideas and discoveries.

Yes, I still believe in miracles, because I have SEEN miracles over these 65 years of living. I have SEEN my beautiful healthy son being born. I have SEEN the gorgeous stars on a clear summer Arkansas night. I have SEEN the brilliant-colored Ozark Mountains in the fall, and I have SEEN the annual miracle spring rebirth every year! I have SEEN ordinary everyday American citizens do extraordinary things many, many times in my life, especially when involved in local political and small business activities. I have SEEN simple and humble folks turn their "American dreams" into "American realities" many times over the years. Through old-fashioned hard work and determination, they never stopped believing in themselves, and they never quit believing in America.

If we continue to embrace our traditional American values as we plow forward into the future just as our ancestors did, I remain optimistic....**and by the grace of God, the United States of America will survive.**

I cannot ever remember a PERFECT America,

but I do remember a BETTER America!